CAMBRIDGE

COMPLETE

KEY
for Schools

Student's Book
without answers

with Online Workbook

Second edition

GW00467905

A2

WITH ONLINE
PRACTICE

David McKeegan

For the revised exam from 2020

Cambridge University Press
www.cambridge.org/elt

Cambridge Assessment English
www.cambridgeenglish.org

Information on this title: www.cambridge.org/9781108539371

First published 2019

20 19 18 17 16 15 14 13 12 11 10 9 8 7 6 5 4 3 2 1

Printed in the United Kingdom by Latimer Trend

A catalogue record for this publication is available from the British Library

ISBN 978-1-108-53937-1 Student's Book without answers with Online Workbook

The publishers have no responsibility for the persistence or accuracy
of URLs for external or third-party internet websites referred to in this publication,
and do not guarantee that any content on such websites is, or will remain,
accurate or appropriate. Information regarding prices, travel timetables, and other
factual information given in this work is correct at the time of first printing but
the publishers do not guarantee the accuracy of such information thereafter.

Contents

Map of the units

Unit title	Reading and Writing	Listening	Speaking
1 Hi, how are you?	**Part 2:** Three English teenagers **Part 6:** an email	**Part 1:** Five short conversations	**Part 1, Phase 1**
2 We're going home	**Part 1:** signs and notices **Part 7:** a short story	**Part 3:** planning a party	**Part 1, Phase 2**
Vocabulary and grammar review Units 1 and 2			
3 Dinner time	**Part 3:** A young chef **Part 5:** completing a short text	**Part 2:** A cake competition	**Part 2, Phase 1**
4 I'm shopping!	**Part 4:** an article about Alek Wek **Part 7:** a short story	**Part 5:** a fashion show	**Part 1, Phase 2**
Vocabulary and grammar review Units 3 and 4			
5 It's my favourite sport!	**Part 3:** an interview with a young gymnast **Part 6:** an email	**Part 4:** short conversations or monologues	**Part 2, Phase 1**
6 Have you got any homework?	**Part 2:** Student life **Part 5:** completing short messages	**Part 3:** starting a new school	**Part 2, Phase 2**
Vocabulary and grammar review Units 5 and 6			
7 Let's go to the museum	**Part 1:** signs and notices **Part 6:** an email	**Part 4:** five short conversations	**Part 2, Phase 1**
8 Did you get my message?	**Part 2:** Three video makers **Part 5:** completing an email	**Part 5:** a computer fair	**Part 1, Phase 2**
Vocabulary and grammar review Units 7 and 8			
9 I love that film!	**Part 4:** Paddington Bear **Part 7:** a short story	**Part 2:** a music concert	**Part 2, Phase 2**
10 It's going to be sunny	**Part 2:** Holiday activities **Part 5:** completing a text	**Part 1:** five short conversations	**Part 1, Phase 2**
Vocabulary and grammar review Units 9 and 10			
11 I like to keep fit	**Part 3:** A young personal trainer **Part 6:** an email	**Part 4:** short conversations and monologues	**Part 2, Phase 1**
12 Have you ever been on a plane?	**Part 1:** signs and notices **Part 7:** a short story	**Part 2:** a park run	**Part 1, Phase 2**
Vocabulary and grammar review Units 11 and 12			
13 What's your hobby?	**Part 3:** A teenage Go player **Part 6:** an email	**Part 3:** Horse-riding lessons	**Part 2, Phases 1 and 2**
14 Keep in touch!	**Part 4:** Skywriting **Part 5:** completing a short text	**Part 5:** discussing website design	**Parts 1 and 2**
Vocabulary and grammar review Units 13 and 14			

...ronunciation	Vocabulary	Grammar
...ord stress in numbers	Numbers Family members	Present simple Adverbs of frequency
...ord stress: two-syllable words	Time Rooms Furniture	Present continuous *have got*
...', /z/, /ɪz/	School lunches Food phrases	Countable and uncountable nouns *How much / many: a few, a little, a lot*
...and /iː/	Clothes and accessories Adjectives Shops	Present continuous and present simple *too* and *enough*
...wa /ə/	Sports *do, play* and *go* with sports Nationalities	Comparatives and superlatives Prepositions of time (*at, in, on*)
...and /f/	School subjects Classroom objects Education verbs	*have to* Object pronouns
...st simple *-ed* endings	Buildings Directions	Past simple Imperatives
...ə / *can't*	Technology verbs Music	Past continuous *can / can't, could / couldn't*
...r forms	Suggesting, accepting and refusing Adjectives	Verbs with *-ing* or *to* infinitive The future with the present simple, present continuous and *will*
...ng to	What's the weather like? Places	*going to* *must / mustn't*
...tences with *if*	Parts of the body What's the matter? (ailments)	First conditional *something, anything, nothing*, etc.
...nd /tʃ/	Means of transport Vehicles Travel verbs	Present perfect *should / shouldn't*
...'v/ /b/	Hobbies Adverbs Jobs	Present perfect with *for* and *since* *may / might*
...ence stress	Communication verbs *-ed / -ing* adjectives	The passive Present perfect with *just, already* and *yet*

Introduction

Who this book is for

Complete Key for Schools is a stimulating and thorough preparation course for students who wish to take the **A2 Key for Schools exam** from **Cambridge Assessment English**. It teaches you the reading, writing, listening and speaking skills which are necessary for the exam, as well as essential grammar and vocabulary. For those who are not planning to take the exam in the near future, the book provides skills and language which are all highly relevant for school-age learners moving towards an A2 level of English.

What the Student's Book contains:

- **14 units for classroom study.** Each unit contains:
  - an authentic exam task taken from each of the three papers in the **Key for Schools exam**. The units provide language input and skills practice to help you deal successfully with the tasks in each part.
  - essential information on what each part of the exam involves, and the best way to approach each task.
  - a wide range of enjoyable and stimulating speaking activities designed to increase your fluency and your ability to express yourself.
  - grammar and vocabulary activities and exercises for the grammar and vocabulary you need to know for the exam. When you are doing these exercises, you will sometimes see this symbol: ⊙ These exercises are based on research from the Cambridge Learner Corpus and they deal with the areas which often cause problems for candidates in the exam.
  - **seven unit reviews**. These contain exercises which revise the grammar and vocabulary that you have studied in each unit.
  - **Speaking and Writing reference sections.** These explain the possible tasks you may have to do in the Speaking and Writing papers, and they give you examples and models together with additional exercises and advice on how best to approach these Speaking and Writing exam tasks.
  - a **Grammar reference section** which clearly explains all the main areas of grammar you will need to know for the **Key for Schools exam**. There are also practice exercises for all grammar points.
  - extra online resources to help you with grammar, vocabulary and exam preparation.

Also available are:

- **Downloadable audio online** containing listening material for the 14 units of the Student's Book plus material for the Speaking Bank. The listening material is indicated by coloured icons 🎧 in the Student's Book.
- A **Teacher's Book** containing:
  - **step-by-step guidance** for handling the activities in the Student's Book.
  - a number of suggestions for **alternative treatments** of activities in the Student's Book and suggestions for **extension activities**.
  - **Photocopiable recording scripts** from the Student's Book listening material.
  - **complete answer keys** including recording scripts for all the listening material. All sections of text which provide answers to listening tasks are underlined.
  - **14 photocopiable word lists** (one for each unit) containing vocabulary found in the units. Each vocabulary item in the word list is accompanied by a definition supplied by the corpus-informed *Cambridge Learner's Dictionary*.
  - **access to extra photocopiable materials online** to practise and extend language abilities outside the requirements of the **Key for Schools exam**.
- A **Workbook** containing:
  - **14 units for homework and self-study.** Each unit contains further exam-style exercises to practise the reading, grammar and vocabulary, which also uses information about common exam candidate errors from the Cambridge Learner Corpus ⊙ .
  - **Vocabulary Extra** sections, at the end of each unit, which contain further revision and practice of the essential **Key for Schools exam** vocabulary in the Student's Book units.
  - downloadable audio online containing all the listening material for the Workbook.
- A **Test Generator** containing:
  - a grammar and vocabulary test at standard and plus levels of each of the 14 units in the Student's Book.
  - three Term Tests including grammar, vocabulary and exam tasks for: writing, speaking, listening and reading
  - an end of year test including grammar and vocabulary from all 14 units along with exam tasks for: writing, speaking, listening and reading.

Part/Timing	Content	Exam focus
Reading and Writing hour	**Part 1:** Discrete three-option multiple choice questions on six short texts. **Part 2:** Matching. There are three short texts with seven items. Candidates are asked to decide which text an item refers to. **Part 3:** Three-option multiple choice. Candidates read a text and are asked to choose the correct answer from five multiple-choice questions. **Part 4:** Three-option multiple-choice cloze. A text is followed by six questions. Candidates select the correct word from each question to complete the text. **Part 5:** Open cloze. Candidates complete gaps in one or two short texts. **Part 6:** Writing – short message **Part 7:** Writing – story	**Part 1:** Candidates focus on overall understanding of emails, notices and messages. **Part 2:** Candidates read for specific information and detailed comprehension. **Part 3:** Candidates read for detailed understanding and main ideas. **Part 4:** Candidates read and identify the appropriate word. **Part 5:** Candidates read and identify the appropriate word with the focus on grammar. **Part 6:** Candidates write a communicative note or email of at least 25 words. **Part 7:** Candidates write a narrative of at least 35 words describing the people, events and locations that are shown in three pictures.
Listening approximately minutes	**Part 1:** Five short dialogues with three-option multiple-choice questions with pictures. **Part 2:** Longer dialogue. Five gaps to fill with words or numbers. **Part 3:** Longer informal dialogue with five three-option multiple-choice items. **Part 4:** Five three-option multiple choice questions on five short dialogues or monologues. **Part 5:** Matching. There is a longer informal dialogue. Candidates match five items with eight options.	**Part 1:** Candidates are expected to listen and identify key information. **Part 2:** Candidates are expected to identify and write down key information. **Part 3:** Candidates listen to identify specific information, feelings and opinions. **Part 4:** Candidates listen to identify the main idea, message, gist, topic or point. **Part 5:** Candidates listen to identify specific information.
Speaking 0 minutes pair of candidates	**Part 1 Phase 1:** Each candidate interacts with the interlocutor, giving factual information of a personal nature. **Part 1 Phase 2:** A topic-based interview where the interlocutor asks each candidate two questions about their daily life. **Part 2 Phase 1:** A discussion based on topic-based artwork prompts. Candidates discuss the objects and activities in the artwork with each other. **Part 2 Phase 2:** The interlocutor leads follow-up discussion on same topic as Phase 1. Each candidate is asked two questions.	**Part 1:** Candidates focus on interactional and social language. **Part 2:** Candidates focus on organising a larger unit of discourse.

1 Hi, how are you?

Starting off

1 What do you see in the photos?

2 Complete the conversation with phrases from the box.

> Do you like school?   I'm 13.   Nice to meet you.
> ~~What's your name?~~

Thiago: Hey. (1) ....*What's your name?*............
Sophie: My name's Sophie.
Thiago: I'm Thiago. (2) ....
How old are you?
Sophie: (3) ....
What about you?
Thiago: I'm 13, too. (4) ....
Sophie: Yes, I do!

3 Listen and check.
02

4 Work in pairs. Practise the conversation.
Give true information about yourself.

Listening Part 1
Numbers

/p/ Word stress

Listen to the numbers. <u>Underline</u> the stressed part.

1	thir<u>teen</u>	<u>thir</u>ty
2	fourteen	forty
3	fifteen	fifty
4	sixteen	sixty
5	seventeen	seventy
6	eighteen	eighty
7	a hundred and nineteen	a hundred and ninety

Listen again and say the numbers.

Listen and circle the numbers you hear.

13	30	17	70
14	40	18	80
15	50	119	190
16	60		

Listen to the conversations. Write down the three numbers you hear in each conversation.

1 ....15........ ....
2 ....
3 ....

- You will hear five short conversations.
- You will hear each conversation twice.
- You must choose the correct picture.

Exam advice

Read question 1, and say the numbers on the doors. Listen and choose the correct answer.

1 Where does Thiago live?

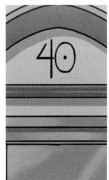

A   B   C

6 Read questions 2–5. <u>Underline</u> the key words. Then describe what you can see in the pictures.

2 Which is Lucy's family?

A   B   C

3 How much is the bag?

A   B   C

4 Which is the girl's bus?

A   B   C

5 Which is Charlotte's favourite photo?

A   B   C

7 Listen. For these questions, choose the correct answer. Then listen again and check.

 07

1

Grammar
Present simple

▶ **Page 106 Grammar reference**
Present simple

> **Rules**
>
> 1 We use the verb *to be* to talk about age, nationality, etc.
> *My brother is 12.*
>
> 2 We use the present simple to talk about things that are always true or things that happen regularly.
> *He's really good at football.*
> *He lives in our street.*

1 Look at the photos. Talk about Adrian and Marcia using words from the box. Then listen and check.

> 13   14   dancing   France   football
> piano   Poland   tennis

Adrian is from Poland. He likes . . .

Adrian

13

Marcia

14

2 Ask and answer questions with *Do …?* and *Are …?*

> Do you like football?
>
> Yes, I do.
>
> Are you from France?
>
> No, I'm not.

3 Complete the sentences with the correct present simple form of the verb in bracke Use short forms.

> My best friend's name **(1)** .... (be) Dexter. He **(2)** ....(not be) from England – he's from America.
> He **(3)** .... (love) sport, especiall football. I **(4)** .... (not like) spor at all, but Dexter and I **(5)** .... (b very good friends. We **(6)** .... (liv in the same street.
>
> Sometimes, I **(7)** .... (go) to his house and watch films. He **(8)** .... (not have) any brothers or sisters. His mur and dad **(9)** .... (be) really nice. They both **(10)** .... (work) at home. They **(11)** .... (be) a very happy family. Have you got a best friend?

4 Work in pairs. Take turns to tell your partner about one of these people. Then ask and answer questions about them. Use the ideas below.

> best friend   brother   father
> mother   sister   teacher

> be funny?   be tall?
> do sport?   like music?

> My best friend is from Spain. She lives in Malaga.

> Is she fun

> Yes, she is.

> Does she do any sp

Vocabulary

Family members

Steve and Mary

Tom and Janet

Gina and Alan

Carl

Megan

Bob

Look at Carl's family tree.
Complete the sentences with words from the box.

> aunt brother cousin daughter granddaughter
> grandad ~~grandma~~ grandson husband sister
> son uncle wife

1 Janet is Carl's ..... *grandma* ..... .
2 Tom is Carl's ....
3 Tom is Janet's ....
4 Janet is Tom's ....
5 Alan is Carl's ....
6 Gina is Carl's ....
7 Bob is Carl's ....
8 Carl is Steve and Mary's ....
9 Megan is Steve and Mary's ....
10 Megan is Carl's ....
11 Carl is Megan's ....
12 Bob is Tom and Janet's ....
13 Megan is Tom and Janet's ....

Work in pairs. Draw your family tree. Ask and answer questions about your partner's tree.

> Who is Alejandro?

> He's my uncle.

Reading Part 2

1 Work in small groups. Discuss the questions. Are you similar or different?

- How old are you?
- Where do you live?
- Who do you live with?
- Do you like sport?
- Do you like music?

2 Reading Part 2 often asks you to find information. Look at these extracts. Who has a brother and sisters?

Ellie: I'm 12 and I live in a city with my parents, my two sisters, Mel and Sue, and my little brother, Mark.

Laura: I live with my mum and dad. I'm nearly 13 and I don't have any brothers or sisters.

Chloe: I'm 13 years old – two years older than my little sister, Monica. … I don't have any brothers … My dad is a mechanic. My mum isn't from England …

3 Look at the questions in Exercise 4 and <u>underline</u> the key words in each question.

4 For each question, choose the correct answer.

	Ellie	Laura	Chloe
1 Who has a <u>brother</u> and <u>sisters</u>?	A	B	C
2 Who doesn't like sport?	A	B	C
3 Who says she wants to go to university?	A	B	C
4 Who is the oldest?	A	B	C
5 Who has a pet?	A	B	C
6 Who has a friend from another country?	A	B	C
7 Who can play a musical instrument?	A	B	C

THREE ENGLISH TEENAGERS

ELLIE

I'm 12 years old and I live in London with my parents, my two sisters Mel and Sue, and my little brother, Mark – oh, and our dog, Rufus! I'm the youngest girl in my family. Mel and Sue are both 19. They are at university. My best friend is called Stef. She's really funny and very good at playing the guitar. She's in a band. They're playing at the school party tonight.

LAURA

I live with my mum and dad in a small town in the north. I'm nearly 13. I don't have any brothers or sisters. My mum is a musician, and my dad teaches at the university. I hope to study there when I'm older. It's my birthday next week and I'm having a party. I'm inviting all my friends. We're having lunch then going to a football match. My best friend Anya is from Poland. She hates sport, but she'll still have fun!

CHLOE

I'm 13 years old – two years older than my little sister, Monica. I don't have any brothers. We live in a big family house in a village. I don't have any pets, but I'd really like a cat! My dad is a mechanic. My mum isn't from England. She's Spanish and she teaches languages at my school. Everyone in my family plays some kind of sport, but I don't like sports very much. All I play is my piano!

Grammar

Adverbs of frequency

▶ **Page 107 Grammar reference**
Adverbs of frequency

1 Look at this information about Ellie's week. Then complete the diagram with the <u>underlined</u> words.

1 Ellie <u>always</u> gets up at 7.00 am.
2 She <u>usually</u> does her homework in the evening.
3 She is <u>never</u> late for school.
4 She <u>often</u> goes shopping on Saturday.
5 She <u>sometimes</u> does the washing-up at home.

........*never*........ ....

1 _____3_____

........2........ ....4........

....

2 Listen and complete the sentences about Stevie.

1 Stevie ....*always*....... gets up at 8 o'clock.
2 He .... does his homework in the mornin
3 He is .... late for school on Mondays.
4 He .... goes shopping on Wednesdays.
5 He .... does the washing-up.

3 Complete the rules with *before* or *after*.

> **Rules**
>
> 1 Adverbs of frequency come .... the verb *to b*
> 2 Adverbs of frequency come .... other verbs.

4 Exam candidates often make mistakes with adverbs frequency. Correct the mistakes in the sentences.

1 I ~~stay often~~ at the beach. *often stay*
2 You are welcome always in my home.
3 I usually can go out with my friends on Saturdays.
4 Our teacher forgets never our homework.
5 My dad goes often to work by bus.
6 I usually am a good student.

5 Write sentences about yourself.

> am happy   am hungry   do sport
> do the washing-up   ride a bike   walk to school

I am always happy on Saturdays. It's the weekend

6 Work in pairs. Ask and answer *How often …?* questi about your sentences from Exercise 5.

peaking Part 1

▶ **Page 146 Speaking Bank**
Speaking Part 1

> • There are two main parts in the Speaking paper.
>
> • In Part 1, you will talk with the examiner for three or four minutes.
>
> • The examiner will first ask you about your name, your age, and where you are from.

Exam advice

What things do you ask a person about when you meet them for the first time?

What's your name?

Match questions 1–6 with answers a–f. Then listen and check.

1 What's your name? *e*
2 Where are you from?
3 How old are you?
4 How many people are in your family?
5 Who in your family do you like spending time with?
6 How often do you meet your friends?

a I'm from São Paulo. In Brazil.
b There are five people.
c I'm 13 years old.
d I like spending time with my grandma.
e My name is Gabriel Silva.
f I meet them every day.

Work in pairs. Ask and answer questions 1–6 from Exercise 2.

Writing Part 6

▶ **Page 139 Writing Bank**
Writing Part 6

> • There are two parts in the Writing test.
>
> • First, you must write a note or an email.
>
> • There are three points you need to write about.
>
> • You must write 25 words or more.

Exam advice

1 **Read this email. Underline the three points you need to write about.**

> ● ● ●
>
> Hi,
>
> My name is Alex. I'm your new pen friend. I've got a little brother, and I love playing football. Have you got any brothers and sisters? What things do you like doing? What kind of music do you like?
>
> Alex

2 **Read two students' answers to the email. Which student answers all the points in Alex's email?**

> ● ● ●
>
> Hello Alex
>
> My name is Juan. I've got three brothers and one sister. I love spending time with my friends and I enjoy sports. I like all kinds of music – but Taylor Swift is my favourite!
>
> Juan

> ● ● ●
>
> Hi Alex
>
> Thanks for your email. My name is Stef and I am your pen friend. Tennis is my favourite sport. I love it. My mother doesn't like it.
>
> Stef

3 **Write your own answer to Alex's email. Write 25 words or more.**

2 We're going home

A

B

C

D

Starting off

1. What kind of home can you see in the photos
   Which one would you like to live in? Why?

2. Work in pairs. Which homes do you think have
   these things?

   > a door   a first floor   a garage   a gate   a lift
   > a roof   stairs   a swimming pool   windows

3. What kind of home do you live in? What does it have?
   Use words from Exercise 2.

Listening Part 3

1. Work in pairs. Look at the
   party invitation.

   1. What kind of party is it?
   2. What time does it start?
   3. Where is the party?

Invitatio

We've got a new h
Come to the Bakers'

Date: July 31
Time: 12.30

Time

Listening Part 3 sometimes has a question about time. Look at the clocks. Match them to the times (1–6).

1 two o'clock
2 quarter past four
3 half past twelve
4 quarter to ten
5 twenty-five to three
6 ten past eight

> • You will hear a conversation between two people.
> • There are five multiple-choice questions.
> • You must choose between three possible answers: A, B or C.
> • The answers may be sentences, numbers or words.
>
> **Exam advice**

For these questions, choose the correct answer. You will hear Jarred talking to his friend Gemma about a party.

1 How does Jarred feel about Jake's party?
   A worried   **B** excited   **C** surprised
2 What time does the party start?
   A 2.00   **B** 2.30   **C** 3.00
3 Rachel is Gemma's
   A cousin   **B** friend   **C** brother
4 The party is at
   A 14 Green Street   **B** 24 Green Street   **C** 40 Green Street
5 What sort of music does Jarred think is best for parties?
   A pop   **B** hip hop   **C** rock

Do you like parties? What do you like doing at parties?

Grammar
Present continuous

▶ **Page 108 Grammar reference**
Present continuous

1 It's Jake's surprise party. Look at the picture. Are these things true (T) or false (F)?

1 Emily is eating a sandwich. T
2 Jenny is writing an email. F
3 Jarred is singing.
4 Suzy is wearing sunglasses.
5 Simon is enjoying the party.
6 Jake and Rachel are dancing.
7 Martin isn't taking a selfie.

2 Choose the correct option in *italics* to complete the rules.

Rules

1 We use the present continuous to talk about things that *are happening now / usually happen*.

2 We form the present continuous with *to be / to have* and the *-ing* form of the verb.

3 Correct the sentences.

1 He is sleeping. (play)

He isn't sleeping.
He's playing.

2 She is writing. (read)

3 She's watching TV.
(listen / to music)

4 They're laughing.
(cry)

4 Listen and tick (✓) the correct answers.

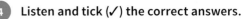

12

1 Is he running?
  A Yes, he is. ✓
  B No, he isn't.
2 Are they dancing?
  A Yes, they are.
  B No, they aren't.
3 Is she typing?
  A Yes, she is.
  B No, she isn't.

4 Is he playing?
  A Yes, he is.
  B No, he isn't.
5 Are they singing?
  A Yes, they are.
  B No, they aren't.

5 Complete the questions. Write true answers.

1 ....*Are*......... you sleeping?
No, I'm not. ....
2 .... you sitting down?
....
3 .... your friends sitting near you?
....
4 .... your teacher helping you?
....
5 .... it raining?
....

6 Student A, look at the picture on Page 149. Student B
look at the picture on page 150. What is different? As
and answer questions.

What's David doing in your picture?

Vocabulary
Rooms

bathroom ~~bedroom~~ dining room garag
garden hall kitchen living room

1 Label the picture of Jake's new house.

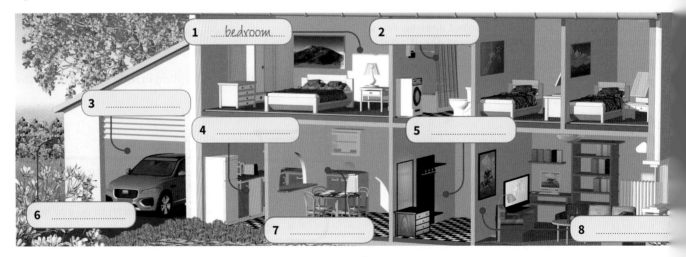

1 ......*bedroom*......
2 ....
3 ....
4 ....
5 ....
6 ....
7 ....
8 ....

2 Listen. What room are they in?

13

3 Work in pairs. Take turns to say what you are doing
Your partner tries to guess what room you are in.

eading Part 1

Mum, I'm in my bedroom and I'm studying.
Can we have dinner at 8 o'clock after I finish all my homework? Thanks.
Ben

A Ben wants to do his homework in the dining room.

B Ben doesn't want dinner before he finishes his homework.

C Ben has got a lot of homework and doesn't want any dinner.

1 Work in pairs. Look at the messages in Exercise 2. Where are they (in a restaurant, on a phone, etc.)?

2 For each question, choose the correct answer.

- You will read short messages (short emails, text messages, notices, emails or labels).

- There are three options. Choose the option which means the same as the short message.

Exam advice

i Steve,
ve got the present for Miguel. It cost $12, so can you give me half
f that when you see me?
hanks,
loe

Chloe wrote this message because

A she wants to borrow money to buy a present.

B she needs ideas about what present to buy.

C she wants to share the cost of a present.

Hi Angela,
Our swimming lesson is at 3 o'clock instead of 3.30.
Mum can pick us up at 2.50. Don't forget your swimming hat,
Dan.

Dan wants Angela to

A take him to swimming classes.

B be ready earlier than usual.

C meet him at the pool.

Seavista Restaurant

Opening this weekend. Free food for children

A The restaurant is old.

B The restaurant has great food.

C Guests don't have to pay for children's meals.

by, Julie's party starts at 5pm, but we have football then.
can go afterwards at about 6pm. Let me know what you think.
e.

What should Toby do now?

A Tell Kyle if he agrees to go to the party late.

B Find out what time the party begins.

C Ask Julie if he can come to the party.

IMPORTANT NOTICE.

Class 5C English is in Room 4 today.
(2.25 start, as usual)

A This lesson is in a different place today.

B This lesson is not happening today.

C This lesson begins a bit later today.

2

Grammar
have got

▶ **Page 109 Grammar reference**
have got

1 **Match the sentences with the pictures.**

1 I've got the present for Miguel.
2 Ben has got a lot of homework.

2 **Choose the correct option in *italics*.**

1 I *have got / has got* blue eyes.
2 My dad *hasn't got / haven't got* dark hair.
3 *Have / Has* you got a big bedroom?
   No, I *haven't / hasn't*.
4 I *hasn't / haven't* got a desk in my room.
5 *Have / Has* your brother got a new smart phone?
   Yes, he *have / has*.
6 This is my cat. It *has / have* got a long tail.

3 **Write five true or false sentences. Read them to your partner. Guess if they are true or false.**

I've got four brothers.

False! You haven't got four brothers.

Yes, I have. It's true!

Vocabulary
Furniture

1 **Label the picture.**

> bed   bookshelf   carpet   chair   curtains
> desk   lamp

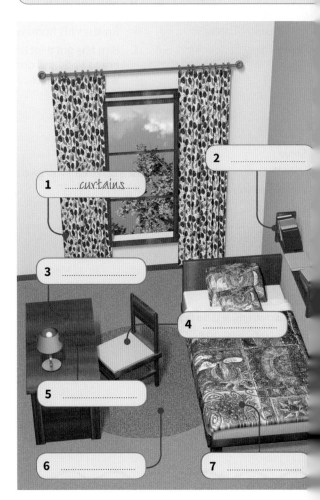

1 ......curtains......
2 ....
3 ....
4 ....
5 ....
6 ....
7 ....

2 **/p/ Word stress (two-syllable words)**

(14) **Listen to the words. Underline the stressed parts.**

bedroom   curtain
bookshelf   kitchen
carpet   table

3 **Listen again and repeat the words.**

(14)

4 **Write sentences to describe your room. Practise say** them to your partner.

I've got red curtains in my bedroom.

peaking Part 1

▶ Page 146 Speaking bank
Speaking Part 1

- In the second part of Speaking Part 1, the examiner will ask two questions about a topic.

- Then, the examiner will say *Please tell me something about* … . You should say at least <u>three</u> things.

Exam advice

Listen to two students doing Speaking Part 1.

1 What does the examiner want to know?
2 How many things does each student say?
3 Which student gives the best answer?

Write three true things for each answer.

1 Please tell me something about your **school**.

It's a big school. It's got a swimming pool.
....
I like it.

2 Please tell me something about your **English teacher**.

His/Her name is ....
....
....

3 Please tell me something about your **favourite hobby**.

My favourite hobby is ....
....
....

4 Please tell me about a nice day you spent with your **family**.

....
....
....

Work in pairs. Discuss the topics from Exercise 2.

Writing Part 7

▶ Page 141 Writing bank
Writing Part 7

- There are three pictures.
- You must write a short story.
- You must write 35 words or more.

Exam advice

1 Work in pairs. Look at the pictures. Write down things you can see.

A  B  C

2 Discuss the questions.

Picture 1
- What do you want to call the boy?
- How old is he?
- Where is he?

Picture 2
- Where is the boy?
- What is he doing?

Picture 3
- Who can you see?
- What are they doing?
- How does the boy feel?

3 Read theses ideas for picture 1. Which idea do you like best? Why?

1 This is Jack. He is 13 years old.
2 One day, Jack walks home from school.
3 Jack is walking home from school.

4 Finish writing the story.

1 Vocabulary and grammar review

Grammar

1 Complete the email with the present simple form of the verbs in brackets.

Hi,

My name (1) ...is... (be) Carla. I (2) .... (live) in England with my family. I (3) .... (have) a brother called Sam. I (4) .... (not have) any sisters. I (5) .... (love) dancing. Sam (6) .... (love) sports, but he (7) .... (not like) school. I think school (8)............................ (be) OK, but I (9) .... (not like) sports. My parents (10) .... (be) teachers. They (11) .... (not work) at our school. I (12) .... (be) happy about that!

Write soon!

Carla

2 Put the frequency adverbs in the correct place.

      never
1 I am ^ late for school. (never)
2 We go shopping in the evening. (often)
3 My dad has breakfast at 7.30 am. (usually)
4 Dan does the washing-up. (never)
5 Do you do your homework in the morning? (often)
6 I watch TV in the evenings. (sometimes)
7 Maths lessons aren't fun. (usually)
8 Soraya is happy! (always)

Vocabulary

3 Complete the number lists.

1 three, four, five, six, ...*seven*........., eight, nine
2 eight, ten, ..., fourteen, sixteen
3 ninety, ..., seventy, sixty, fifty
4 twenty, ..., thirty, thirty-five, forty
5 thirteen, twelve, ..., ten, nine, eight
6 one hundred, one hundred and ten, ..., one hundred and thirty
7 twenty-two, thirty-three, ..., fifty-five
8 three, six, nine, twelve, ..., eighteen

4 Complete the crossword with family members.

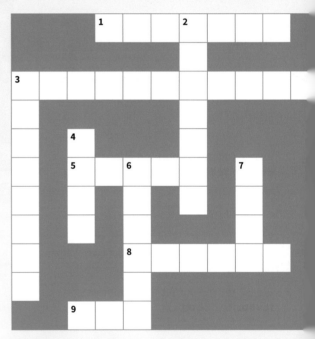

Across
1 My father is my mother's ...
3 My mother's mother.
5 My dad's brother.
8 My parents' daughter.
9 My brother is my mother's ...

Down
2 My parents' son.
3 My brother is my grandfather's ...
4 My mother's sister.
6 My uncle's daughter.
7 My mother is my father's ...

Grammar

Put the words in the correct order.

1 three brothers / has / Greg / got
   Greg has got three brothers.

2 haven't / your / I / got / pen
   ....

3 got / All my friends / laptops / have
   ....

4 black hair / My grandfather / got / hasn't
   ....

5 got / You / a nice room / have
   ....

6 you / my book / Have / got ?
   ....

7 got / a car / We / haven't
   ....

8 sister / a big desk / got / Has / your ?
   ....

Look at the pictures. What are the people doing? Write sentences using words from the box.

> laugh   listen to music   play football
> read a book   swim   write a story

1 She's listening to music.   2 ....

3 ....   4 ....

5 ....   6 ....

Vocabulary

3 **Look at the clocks. Write the times.**

1 ....quarter to four....   2 ....

3 ....   4 ....

5 ....   6 ....

4 **Put the words in the correct order to make words for rooms and furniture.**

Rooms

1 LAHL   ....hall....
2 MOTHBORA   ....
3 THICNEK   ....
4 MOREBOD   ....

Furniture

5 DEB   ....
6 SKED   ....
7 HARCI   ....
8 BETAL   ....

3 Dinner time

1 Work in pairs. What types of food can you see in the photos? Write down the English words that you know.

fruit and vegetables

meat and fish

dairy

other types of food

2 Which food in the photos do you like best? Which is healthy?

3 What is your favourite meal? Find someone in your class who has the same favourite meal as you.

Reading Part 3

- Reading Part 3 tests your understanding of a long text.
- There are five multiple-choice questions.
- You must choose between three possible answers: A, B or C.

Exa
advi

1 Work in pairs.
- Do you know any recipes?
- Do you help in the kitchen? What do you do?

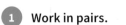

recipe (*noun*) a set of instructions telling you how prepare and cook food, including a list of what foo need for this

Young chef

14-year-old Marc Weiner has his own cooking show on TV.

Marc, when did you start cooking?

I started helping my mum in the kitchen when I was six. I made her coffee – it was terrible! I was seven when I made my first meal – a pizza with four different kinds of cheese.

Do you have a favourite recipe?

It's hard because I have so many. The easy ones are fun – things with pasta, tomatoes and onions. My favourites are the ones that include fish. There are so many different things you can do!

What do your parents think of your cooking?

When I won my first competition, my mum and dad understood that I was a real chef. They're glad that they don't have to make dinner every night, and they enjoy my food – usually! But, you can't make everyone happy all the time.

What's the best way to get good at cooking?

First, I threw away some of what I made because it was no good. That's how you learn. Then, I did it differently the next time. You need to practise, so if you know a chef, ask if you can help them in the kitchen sometimes.

Finally, what's it like being on TV?

It's interesting. I'm actually a very quiet person, so I'm amazed that I really enjoy myself making the shows. They're watched by millions, but I still find it strange when people I don't know say hello to me in the street.

For each question, choose the correct answer.

1 How old was Marc when he started cooking?
   A four
   B six
   C seven

2 Marc says that his favourite recipes
   A use one kind of food.
   B are easy to make.
   C include a variety of vegetables.

3 What does Marc say about his parents?
   A They are happy that he wins prizes for cooking.
   B They get bored of cooking the same things.
   C They don't always like his cooking.

4 What does Marc think is the best way to improve?
   A Cook every day.
   B Go to cooking classes.
   C Learn from your mistakes.

5 How does Marc feel about having a TV show?
   A happy that he is now famous
   B surprised at how much fun it is
   C excited by talking to so many people

School lunches

1 Label the lunches with the words from the box.

> apple   banana   biscuits   cake   cheese   chicken
> ice cream   lemonade   orange juice
> ~~sandwiches~~   salad   rice   water

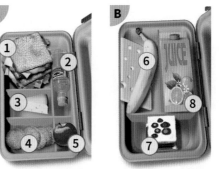

A   B   C

1	...sandwiches...	8	....
2	....	9	....
3	....	10	....
4	....	11	....
5	....	12	....
6	....	13	....
7	....		

2 Listen to three students talking about their school lunches. Match the names with lunches A–C in Exercise 1.

16

Becky ....
Murray ....
Tina ....

3 Work in pairs. Say what you have for lunch at school. Use adverbs of frequency (*always, usually, sometimes*, etc.).

4 /**P**/ / s /, / z /, / ɪz /

17

Listen and underline the end-of-word -s in each word. Notice how they sound different.
Murray likes his mum's chicken sandwiches.

5 Listen and complete the table with words from the box.

18

> apples   chips   dishes   fridges   onions   wants

/s/	/z/	/ɪz/
likes	mum's	sandwiches

3

Grammar
Countable and uncountable nouns

▶ **Page 110 Grammar reference**
Countable and uncountable nouns

1 Mia and Noah are shopping for food. Look at what they've got in their shopping baskets and read the statements. Whose basket is full of countable food? Whose is full of uncountable food?

A

B

Mia: I've got some cheese, butter, orange juice and chocolate in my basket.

Noah: I've got three tomatoes, an onion, four carrots, and six eggs in my basket.

2 Complete the rules with *Countable* or *Uncountable*.

> **Rules**
>
> • .... nouns do not take *a/an* or a number.
> • .... nouns have a singular and a plural form.
> • .... nouns do not have a plural form.
> • .... nouns can take *a/an* or a number.

3 Complete the table with the words from the box.

> biscuit ~~bread~~ ~~burger~~ chips grape
> milk rice tea

countable	uncountable
burger	bread

4 Read the conversation. Then complete the rules with *some* or *any*.

Noah: Hi Mum, it's Noah. I'm in the supermarket. Have we got any cheese in the fridge?

Mum: Let me see… yes, we've got some cheese.

Noah: Have we got any lemons?

Mum: No, we haven't got any lemons. Can you get two or three, please?

Noah: Sure. Would you like me to get some chocolate?

Mum: No, thanks. But could you get some biscuits?

Noah: OK.

> **Rules**
>
> 1 We usually use .... in positive sentences, offer and requests.
>
> 2 We usually use .... in negative sentences and in questions.

5 Complete the conversation with *a/an*, *some* or *any*. Then listen and check answers.

19

Mia: Dad, I'm hungry.

Dad: Would you like **(1)** .... apple?

Mia: No, thanks. I don't like apples. Can I have **(2)** .... cheese?

Dad: No, we haven't got **(3)** ...., I'm afraid.

Mia: Have we got **(4)** .... biscuits?

Dad: Oh yes. There are **(5)** .... in the cupbo...

Mia: Great! I'll have **(6)** .... biscuit, then!

Dad: Me too!

6 Exam candidates often make mistakes with *a/an*, *some* and *any*. Correct the mistake in each sentence.

1 Can I have a orange?
2 On Sundays, we have great time together.
3 I start a work at eight o'clock.
4 I bought a black trousers and a pink T-shirt.
5 Don't forget to buy a milk.
6 Do you know shops near here?

7 Work in pairs. Choose three things to eat and three things to drink from this section. Write them on a pi... of paper. Take turns to offer your partner something...

> Would you like some milk?

> No, thanks. I don't like milk. Have you got any...

Listening Part 2

How often do you eat cake? Do you eat it when you have a special day?

- In Listening Part 2, you will hear one person.
- There are five questions and an example.
- You must write five pieces of information to complete the notes.
- The information can be a number, time, date, word or spelling.

Exam advice

Match questions 1–5 in Exercise 3 with the answers (a–f).

a a day or date ○
b food
c a person's name
d number
e time
f prize

For these questions, write the correct answer in each gap. You will hear a teacher talking to her class about a cake competition. Write one word or a number or a date or a time.

Cake Competition

en: (0) Monday 3rd May
e: (1) ....
ere: (2) Room number ....
es must include: (3) flour, butter, sugar and
....
re information from: (4) Mrs ....
ze: (5) ....

Grammar

How much / many; a few a little a lot of

▶ **Page 111 Grammar reference**
How much / many; a few; a little; a lot of

1 Mia wants to enter the cake competition. Listen and complete the conversation with words from the box.

🎧 21

> a few (x2)   a little   a lot   much   ~~many~~

Mia: I want to make a cake for the cake competition.
Dad: What do you need?
Mia: Let's see … eggs.
Dad: How (1) ....*many*........ do you need?
Mia: Just (2) ....! Three, I think.
I also need (3) .... milk for my recipe.
Dad: How (4) .... do you need?
Mia: I don't need (5) .... of milk. Just half a cup. And it's a lemon cake, so I think I'll need (6) .... lemons.
Dad: Really? How (7) ....?
Mia: Let me see – oh, actually I only need one.

2 Which phases from Exercise 1 can we use with countable nouns? Which can we use with uncountable nouns?

3 Choose the correct options in *italics*.

1 **A:** How *many / much* chocolate have we got?
   B: We've got *much / a lot of* chocolate left.
2 **A:** How *many / much* juice is in the fridge?
   B: Just *a little / a few*. Leave some for me.
3 **A:** How *many / much* apples do you eat in a week?
   B: *A few / A little*. About three.
4 **A:** How *many / much* brothers have you got?
   B: I've got seven.
   A: That's *a little / a lot of* brothers!
5 **A:** How *many / much* sandwiches do you want?
   B: Just *a few / a little*, please. I'm not very hungry.

4 Work in pairs. Ask questions with *How much/many*. Use the ideas in the table and *a few, a little, a lot of*.

> How many aunts and uncles have you got?

> I've got a lot of aunts, but I haven't got any uncles.

have got?	eat	drink?
friends	fruit	milk
books	biscuits	bottles of water
music	chocolate	tea

Vocabulary
Food phrases

1 Look at the menu. What would you like to eat and drink?

Breakfast menu

cereal   sausage
cheese   cake
toast   fruit

Drinks

tea   water
juice   milk B
coffee

2 Listen to three people talking about breakfast. Write
B (Becky), **T** (Tina) or **M** (Murray) next to each menu item.

3 Look at the photos. Use the words in the circles to say
what you can see.

a

plate
bowl   box
slice   cup   can   of
glass
bottle

bread
tea   cereal
fruit   meat   cola
cake   water
milk

Reading Part 5

4 How many other food phrases can you make?

a bowl of cereal, a cup of coffee . . .

5 Work in pairs. Tell your partner what you usually
have for breakfast.

I usually have a slice of toast and . . .

- You must complete a short email
  or message.
- There are six missing words.
- You must write one word in
  each space.
- You must spell the word
  correctly.

Exam
advice

1 Read the text below quickly. What kind of text is

2 Work in pairs. Look carefully at the words befor
after each gap. What kind of word fits each gap?

- a verb, e.g. *know, like, be …*
- a quantifier, e.g. *many, a few, a little*
- a preposition, e.g. *on, of, at …*
- a pronoun, e.g. *I, you, me …*
- a question word, e.g. *When, What, How …*

3 For each question, write the correct answer.
Write one word for each gap.

Hi Sue,

It's my birthday **(0)** ....on.......... Friday. Would you
(1) .... to come to my house for dinner? N
parents say I can invite a **(2)** .... friends.
Tom and Sophie **(3)** .... coming. It's goin
to be fun! **(4)** .... time can you get to my
house?

You don't have to bring anything . There will be lots
(5) .... cake and lemonade!

I hope you can come. Please call me **(6)** ....
my phone when you have time.

Love,

Teri

peaking Part 2

▶ **Page 147 Speaking bank**
Speaking Part 2

▶ **Page 147 Speaking bank**
Speaking Part 2

> - In Speaking Part 2, you must talk to your partner.
> - The examiner gives you some pictures and a question.
> - You and your partner talk together for about two minutes.

Exam advice

Work in pairs. Which things can you see in the pictures?

> beach   home   fast food place   restaurant   school

Do you like eating in these different places?

2 Now listen to two students talking about one of the pictures. Which picture are they talking about?

3 Write one question about each picture. Use *Do you like … ?* and *Do you think … ?*

Do you like eating in restaurants?
Do you think picnics are fun?

4 Look at this part of the conversation and complete the rules.

A: Do you like eating in restaurants?
B: Yes, I do.
A: Why?
B: Because restaurants have usually got different kinds of food. What do you think?
A: I don't like restaurants.
B: Why not?
A: Because …

Rules

1 We use *Why / Why not* to ask follow-up questions to **positive** statements.

2 We use *Why / Why not* to ask follow-up questions to **negative** statements.

5 Write *Why?* or *Why not?* after each statement.

1 I don't like fast food. *Why not?*
2 I think picnics are fun. ....
3 My brother doesn't like school lunches. ....
4 I love my grandparents' cooking. ....
5 I don't like British food. ....

6 Work in pairs. Ask your questions from Exercise 3. Ask follow-up questions like *Why? / Why not?*

7 Look again at the pictures from Exercise 1. Which do you think is the best place to eat?

4 I'm shopping!

Clothes and accessories

1 Look at the pictures. Where are the people?

2 Match the words (1–12) with the clothes in the pictures.

1	belt *C*	**7**	shirt
2	boots	**8**	shoes
3	dress	**9**	coat
4	hat	**10**	trousers
5	jacket	**11**	sweater
6	jeans	**12**	sunglasses

3 Work in pairs.
- How often do you go shopping for clothes? Do you like it? Why? / Why not?
- Where do you usually buy your clothes?
- Do you wear a school uniform?
- What do you usually wear at the weekend?
- What's your friend wearing today?

Listening Part 5

1 Look at the information below.
1 Where is the fashion show?
2 Where do the clothes come from?
3 Who are the models?

Park Hill School
Fashion Show

Tickets £5

Friday 5th May, 5.30–6.30
Come and see student models wearing the latest fashions from local clothes shops.

Listen to the first part of a conversation. Which item of clothing is Pip wearing?

Exam advice

- You must match the things in the list on the right (A–H) with the words or names in the list on the left (1–5).
- Two of the words in A–H are not used.

For these questions, choose the correct answer. You will hear Pip and Sara talking. What is each person wearing?

Then listen again and check.

People		Clothes	
0	Pip	A	belt
1	Ben	B	boots
2	Amy	C	coat
3	George	D	dress
4	Alice	E	hat
5	Katy	F	jacket
		G	jeans
		H	sweater

Grammar

Present continuous and present simple

▶ **Page 112 Grammar reference**
Present continuous and present simple

Read the online chat. Underline the present continuous verbs, and circle the present simple verbs.

George Jones
is enjoying the school fashion show. 🙂

Jake Thomas
Cool. Are you a model? Or are you watching?

George Jones
I'm a model!

Madison Green
What are you wearing, George?

George Jones
I'm wearing a suit. Look.

Jake Thomas
Ha ha! You look funny. Now I know why you usually wear jeans and a T-shirt.

Madison Green
I think you look great, George.

2 Match rules 1–3 with examples a–c.

Rules

1 We use the present simple to talk about things and actions that happen a lot, or usually.
2 We also use present simple verbs to talk about states that don't change (<u>not</u> actions).
3 We also use the present continuous to talk about things that are happening now.
a I'm wearing a suit.
b You usually wear jeans and a T-shirt.
c I think you look great.

3 Choose the correct option in *italics*.

1 Listen! Olivia *plays / is playing* the guitar.
2 I *don't usually wear / 'm not usually wearing* jeans.
3 *Do you know / Are you knowing* my sister?
4 We *have / 're having* a great time on holiday this week.
5 I *don't understand / am not understanding* this.
6 Bella can't speak now. She *has / is having* her dinner at the moment.

4 Complete the questions.

1 What music / you / usually / listen to ?
What music do you usually listen to?
2 your dad / often / wear / jeans ?
3 you / enjoy / this exercise ?
4 What time / you / usually /go to bed ?
5 What / you / think about / at the moment ?
6 What / the teacher / do / now ?

5 Work in pairs. Ask and answer the questions.

What music do you usually listen to?

I usually listen to pop music.

4

Vocabulary
Adjectives

1 Match the adjectives with their opposites.

> dirty   expensive   light   new   short   small

> cheap   clean   dark   large   long   old

dirty — clean

2 Complete the sentences with adjectives from Exercise 1.

1 My jacket was only €3. That's very *cheap*!

2 These gloves are very .... I need new ones.

3 I can't put this sweater on. It's really ....

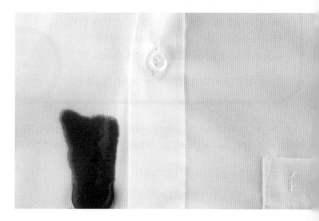

4 This shirt is ....

5 When you ride your bike at night, it is not safe to wear .... colours.

6 €30 for a pair of socks? That's ....!

3 Look around the room. Write three true sentences a
one false sentence about what you see. Use adjectiv
from Exercise 1.

The teacher is wearing a new jacket.

eading Part 4

Look at the photos of Alek Wek. Who do you think she is? What is she doing?

Read the article below quickly and answer the questions.

1 Where is Alek Wek from?
2 Where did she study?
3 What does she do now?

- Reading Part 4 mostly tests vocabulary.
- You must complete a short text.
- You must choose the correct answer (A, B or C) for each space.

Exam advice

3 Look at the sentences in the article about Alek Wek. Try to fill the gaps without looking at options A, B or C. Use these questions to help you.

Gap 1: Do you think her life was *easy*?
Gap 2: What word do you use to say *how old* someone is?
Gap 3: Do good students learn *slowly*?
Gap 4: What word do you use *to get* money by working?
Gap 5: Think of a word that goes with *very*.
Gap 6: Think of a word that is about time.

4 Read the article about Alek Wek again. For each question, choose the correct answer.

		A	B	C
1	A	difficult	B heavy	C wrong
2	A	age	B year	C time
3	A	early	B quickly	C already
4	A	earn	B win	C pay
5	A	excellent	B favourite	C beautiful
6	A	far	B long	C wide

Alek Wek

Alek Wek was born in South Sudan in 1977. She had a
(1) .... life there because there was a war. At the
(2) .... of 14, she left her family in Sudan and
moved to London to live with her sister.

Alek learned English very **(3)** .... She was a
good student, and she also worked hard after school to
(4) .... money which she sent home to her mother.
When she was eighteen she went to college and studied fashion,
technology and business.

She was very **(5)** .... and one day a person from a
model agency saw her in the street and asked her to work for
them. It wasn't **(6)** .... before she became a rich and
famous model. Now she works to help people in South Sudan.

4

Grammar

too and *enough*

▶ **Page 112 Grammar reference**
too and *enough*

1 Read and listen to a conversation in a shop. Complete the conversation with one word in each gap.

🎧 26

Girl: Oh dear. I think this hat is too (1) ....

Assistant: You're right. It isn't (2) .... enough for you.

2 Complete the rules with *too* or *enough*.

Rules

1 We use .... before the adjective.
2 We use .... after the adjective.

3 Complete the sentences with an adjective from the box and *too* or *enough*.

clean ~~cold~~ expensive fast heavy old

1 Look at the snow! It's ......too cold...... to go out today.
2 Sam is only 12. She isn't .... to drive a car.
3 I can't carry this. It's ....
4 He isn't .... to win this race.
5 I can't buy that jacket because I've only got £10. It's ....
6 You can't wear those jeans. They aren't ....

4 Work in pairs. Imagine you want to buy a birthday present for your friend. Use *too* or (*not*) *enough* to say what is wrong with these ideas.

a banana   a horse   a house   a new laptop

I want to buy a horse for my friend.   No, a horse is too big.

Vocabulary

Shops

1 Where can you buy the things in the pictures?

bookshop   chemist   department store   supermarke

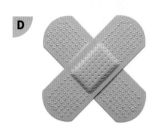

2 What other things can you buy in these shops?

3 Work in pairs. How often do you visit these shops? W do you usually buy there?

4 /p/ /ɪ/ and /iː/

🎧 27

Listen to this sentence. Underline the /ɪ/ sounds and circle the /iː/ sounds.

We like the cheese shop. It's next to the chemist.

5 Listen to these words. Underline the two words whi have the same /ɪ/ or /iː/ sound.

🎧 28

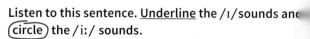

1 free	expensive	clean
2 jeans	jacket	T-shirt
3 department store	swimsuit	cheap
4 aspirin	beans	big

Speaking Part 1

▶ **Page 146 Speaking bank**
Speaking Part 1

Read the exam questions. What words do you think go in the gaps? Listen and check.

- Now, let's talk about **(1)** ....
  What clothes do you wear at the
  (2) .... ?
- What **(3)** .... clothes do you like to wear?
- What clothes do you wear to
  (4) .... ? **(5)** .... helps you buy your clothes?
- Now, please tell me something about the clothes you like to wear to a
  (6) ....

Listen to Maria and Marco. Tick (✓) the correct answers in the table.

Who …?	Maria	Marco
1 answers the questions	☐	☐
2 gives full answers, not only simple words	☐	☐
3 is the best speaker	☐	☐

Work in pairs. Ask and answer the questions from Exercise 1.

Writing Part 7

▶ **Page 141 Writing bank**
Writing Part 7

Look at the three pictures. What can you see?

2️⃣ **Read the first part of the story. Add the correct punctuation to make two sentences.**

noah is in the park hes feeling hot and wants to go in the pool

3️⃣ **Answer the questions in complete sentences to help you write the rest of the story. Remember to use correct punctuation!**

Picture 2
What happens while Noah is swimming?

....

Picture 3
What does Noah do when he gets out of the lake?
How many shoes has he got?

....

How does his mother feel?

....

Grammar

1 Circle the correct option in *italics*.

1 Have we got any (bread) / breads?
2 Here's *an* / *some* apple.
3 There's *a* / *some* dog in the garden.
4 Would you like *a* / *some* cheese?
5 We haven't got *some* / *any* lemonade.
6 Is there any *milk* / *milks* in the fridge?

2 Write questions with *How much* or *How many*.

1 How many sisters have you got?
  I've got 2 sisters.
2 ....
  There's one litre of milk in the fridge.
3 ....
  I drink two bottles of water every day.
4 ....
  There are 22 students in class 3B.
5 ....
  She eats a lot of chocolate.
6 ....
  I haven't got any money.

3 Choose the correct option (A, B or C).

1 I think this soup needs ...... a little ...... salt.
  A a little   **B** a lot   **C** a few
2 Daniel knows .... of people!
  A a little   **B** a lot   **C** a few
3 Can I have .... biscuits, please?
  A a little   **B** a lot   **C** a few
4 Do you want .... cheese on your pasta?
  A a little   **B** a lot   **C** a few
5 Quick! We haven't got .... of time.
  A a little   **B** a few   **C** a lot

4 Exam candidates often make mistakes with countable nouns. Correct the mistake in each sentence.

1 There ~~are~~ a lot of food on the table. is
2 Can I have a pencil and a paper? ....
3 I want to buy some new T-shirt. ....
4 My house has seven room. ....
5 Do we have a bread? ....
6 We haven't got any homeworks tonight! ....

Vocabulary

5 Label the pictures. Use *a/an* or *some*.

1 ...... some sandwiches ......

2 ....

3 ....

4 ....

5 ....

6 ....

6 Choose the odd one out.

1 apple   mushroom   (juice)   grape
2 ice cream   tea   lemonade   water
3 onion   fish   carrot   tomato
4 sausage   bacon   burger   biscuit
5 cake   chocolate   pizza   ice cream
6 meat   milk   cheese   butter

7 Complete the food diary with words from the box.

> cups   plate   bottles   bowl (x2)
> ~~slices~~   pieces

WEDNESDAY

Breakfast:	two (1) ...... slices ...... of toast
	one (2) .... of cereal
	two (3) .... of coffee
Lunch:	a (4) .... of meat with salad
	two (5) .... of mineral water
Dinner:	one (6) .... of soup
	one pizza
	three (7) .... of cake

Grammar

Choose the correct option in *italics*.

Hi, Maria

I **(1)** *am* / *am being* very happy that you are my new friend. I **(2)** *am* / *am being* 14 years old and I **(3)** *live* / *am living* in London. I **(4)** *love* / *am loving* music. At the moment I **(5)** *listen* / *'m listening* to the new Little Mix album. I always **(6)** *listen* / *am listening* to music when I am at home.
(7) *Do you like* / *Are you liking* music? I **(8)** *send* / *'m sending* you some photos of my family now. Please send me some of yours.

Jenny

Complete the sentences with the present simple or present continuous form of the verbs in brackets.

1 Simone ....*plays*........ (play) football every day.
2 Look! Your father .... (dance)!
3 I .... (not understand) this question.
4 That's strange. Martin .... (not wear) socks today.
5 .... (you / like) my new boots?
6 What .... (Leila / read) now?

Rewrite the sentences. Use *too* or *enough* and the adjective in brackets.

1 This shirt is too small. (large)
   This shirt isn't large enough.
2 I'm not tall enough. (short)
   ....
3 These exercises are too easy. (hard)
   ....
4 It isn't safe enough. (dangerous)
   ....
5 The end of this film is too sad. (happy)
   ....
6 This car is too slow. (fast)
   ....

Vocabulary

4 **Complete the sentences with the opposite of the <u>underlined</u> adjectives.**

1 Our new car isn't <u>large</u>. It's ....*small*........ .
2 That isn't <u>cheap</u>! It's ....
3 This room is .... It isn't <u>dark</u>.
4 Put on a <u>clean</u> pair of jeans. Those are too ....
5 My bike is really <u>old</u>. Can I get a .... one for my birthday?
6 Sam's hair is very .... I prefer it <u>short</u>.

5 **Complete the words to make items of clothing or shops.**

1 h a t
2 _ h _ _ t
3 _ o _ k _ _ o _
4 _ _ _ _ ser _
5 tra _ _ _ _ s
6 _ _ _ ss
7 s _ _ _ r _ a _ k _ _
8 s _ c _ s
9 _ w _ _ t _ r
10 _ _ e _ i _ t
11 _ _ _ hts
12 j _ c _ e _

5 It's my favourite sport!

A

B

C

D

Starting off

1 Match the sports with the photos.

badminton   basketball   football   judo   table tennis

2 Work in pairs. Do you know the English words for any other sports? Make a list.

3 Tom is interviewing people about sports. Listen and complete the table with the person's favourite.

31

Xuan	Paulo

4 Work in pairs. What is your favourite sport? Why? Where do you play it? How often do you play?

eading Part 3

- Read the title and look at any pictures to get an idea of what the text is about.
- Then read the text carefully

Look at the definition of *train*. Do you train? What sport do you train for?

> *train* /treɪn/ *verb* SPORT [I, T]
> to practise a sport or exercise, often to prepare for a competition

Look at the photo of a gymnast. Do you like watching gymnastics? Do you do gymnastics in school?

Read the interview. For each question, choose the correct answer.

1 Joanna enjoys running in the morning because she likes to
   A   get up early.
   B   talk with her friends.
   C   be alone in the morning.

2 How does Joanna feel about training at the gym?
   A   She's worried about the number of hours she spends there.
   B   She's pleased she does a variety of activities there.
   C   She's glad she doesn't need to go there every day.

3 What does Joanna say about school?
   A   She has too much work to do.
   B   She doesn't like her teachers.
   C   It's a pity that she can't go more often.

4 What does Joanna say about her family?
   A   They enjoy spending time together.
   B   They all like sport.
   C   They help with her homework.

5 Where does she usually meet her friends?
   A   At the bus stop.
   B   In town.
   C   In a café.

Grammar
Comparatives and superlatives

▶ **Page 113 Grammar reference:** comparatives and superlatives

1 Complete the conversation between Chris and Sally with words from the box. Listen and check.

> best   ~~better~~   cooler   faster   harder
> interesting   popular

Chris: Why do you like football so much? Basketball is (1) .... *better* .... !

Sally: No, it isn't. Football is the (2) .... game in the world.

Chris: But basketball is (3) .... and more exciting.

Sally: You're joking! Football is a much more (4) .... game than basketball.

Chris: Ha ha! Why do so many football games finish 0–0?

Sally: Because scoring a goal is (5) .... than scoring a basket.

Chris: In basketball, they often score more than 60 points in one game!

Sally: Yes, I know. But football is the most (6) .... game in the world.

Chris: I don't understand why! Basketball is (7) ....

anna Middleton — a young gymnast

o you have to train a lot, Joanna?
s! I usually get up at 6 o'clock and go running. I don't run
ith my friends. It's great to have some time to myself in the
orning. After that, I have breakfast. Then Dad takes me to
e gym. I train for 20 hours over six days and rest on Sunday.
ften spend full days at the gym. I do different things there.
ometimes I dance or do other exercises. I like it because every
y there's something different to do.

it difficult to do your school work as well?
s, it is. My teachers are lovely and they know the situation.
s true that I'm not at school every day. But I try to do as much
ork as I can. I'm sad that I can't spend more time with my
assmates. They're fun.

What do you do in your free time?
I love being with my family. My brother also does sport – for
him it's football – but we both have Sunday afternoons free.
So we often go for picnics with Mum and Dad in the mountains
near my home. We also like watching TV together, and of
course, I always have homework to do.

Tell us more about the things you like.
My friends and I like shopping! I live in a village, so I get the
bus to town and meet them there. Then we visit our favourite
shops and we usually have a hot chocolate.

5

2 Match the rules (1–2) with the examples (a–b).

Rules

1 We can use *comparatives* to compare one person or thing to another.

2 We can use *superlatives* to compare one person or thing to everything in its group.

a Football is <u>the best</u> game in the world.

b Scoring a goal is <u>harder than</u> scoring a basket.

3 Exam candidates often make mistakes with comparatives and superlatives. Correct the mistakes in each of these sentences.

the most

1 Rugby is ~~the more~~ exciting sport for me.

2 We can go to the sports centre by car because it's more fast.

3 I liked the tennis match because it was between the better players in the world.

4 Jo is slowest runner in the class.

5 Football is the sport most popular in the world – everybody likes it.

6 Snowboarding is more easier to learn than windsurfing.

4 **/P/ schwa /ə/**
33 **Listen to these sentences. Notice the schwa /ə/ sound in the <u>underlined</u> letters. Then listen and repeat again.**

Basketball is bett<u>er</u>.

Scoring <u>a</u> goal is hard<u>er</u> th<u>a</u>n scoring <u>a</u> basket.

5 <u>Underline</u> the schwa /ə/ sound in these sentences.
34 **Listen and check.**

1 I'm a faster runner than your brother.

2 Mike is a better basketball player than me.

6 **Work in pairs. Think of your favourite things. Then say why you think your favourites are better than your partner's.**

> book   sport   sports team   school subject
> TV show   singer

What is your favourite school subject?

Maths. I think it's easy. What is your favourite?

English. It's easier than maths!

For me, maths is the easiest subject!

Vocabulary
do, play and *go* with sports

1 **Match the sentences (1–3) with the photos (A–C).**

1 We <u>play</u> cricket in the summer.

2 They're <u>doing</u> karate.

3 She <u>goes</u> climbing every weekend.

A

B

C

Look at the table. Then complete the rules.

play	do	go
cricket	karate	climbing
hockey	gymnastics	skating

Rules

We use .... with ball games and team sports.

We use .... with sports and activities ending in -ing.

We use .... with non-team sports and activities.

Put these sports and activities in the correct column in the table in Exercise 2.

baseball   judo   running   surfing   volleyball   yoga

Work in pairs. Ask your partner what sports they do.

Do you play football?

Yes, I do. I train on Wednesday and play on Sunday.

Do you do yoga?

No, I don't. My mum does yoga on Saturdays with her friends.

Which is your favourite sport?

Running, because it's cheaper than other sports. What about you?

istening Part 4

- You will hear five short monologues or conversations.
- There is a question for each conversation.

Exam advice

- You have to choose the best answer.

Look at the first question and underline the key words.

1 You will hear a girl talking to her friend about a pair of shoes. Why does she buy them?
   A Because they are comfortable.
   B Because she likes the colour.
   C Because they are good for sports.

Listen to the conversation. Answer the questions.

35

1 Who says the word *comfortable*?
2 Does anyone like the colour very much?
3 What are the shoes for?

3 **Listen again. Choose the correct answer in Exercise 1 (A, B or C).**

35

4 **Underline the key words in questions 2–5. Listen, and for these questions, choose the correct answer.**

36

2 You will hear a football manager talking to his team at half-time. What does he want them to do?
   A Keep the ball for longer.
   B Try harder to get the ball.
   C Run faster with the ball.

3 You will hear a woman talking to her son. Why doesn't she want him to go out?
   A Because she wants him to eat first.
   B Because it's not light enough.
   C Because the weather is bad.

4 You will hear a woman talking about surfing. What advice does she give to someone who wants to start the sport?
   A Don't try to learn without a teacher.
   B Don't spend too much money on a board.
   C Don't think that it is easy to learn.

5 You will hear a girl talking about running. While she's training, what does she think about?
   A Running as fast as possible.
   B How to win the next race.
   C Many different things.

It's my favourite sport!

5

Grammar
Prepositions of time: *at, in, on*

▶ **Page 114 Grammar reference**
Prepositions of time

1 **Read about a swimmer. How often does she train?**

<u>On</u> the 6th August, 2016, Yusra Mardini won her first race at the Rio Olympic Games. She swims in a style called 'butterfly', and she is one of the fastest swimmers in the world.

Yusra is a Syrian refugee who lives in Germany now. When she was at the Rio Olympics, she was in a team of other refugees. She hopes to compete again <u>in</u> 2020, when the Olympics are in Japan. She says she wants to make all refugees proud of her.

Every morning, she wakes up <u>at</u> 6 o'clock in the morning and goes to the pool to train. 'When I swim,' she says, 'It's the best feeling in the world'. She trains again <u>in</u> the afternoon and <u>at</u> the weekend, too. It's hard work, but she loves it!

refugee /ref.juˈdʒiː/ *noun*
a person who leaves their own country because of a war or other reasons

2 **Complete the rules with <u>underlined</u> words from the text.**

Rules

1 We use .... with clock times, meals, festivals and *the weekend*.

2 We use .... with parts of the day (the *morning*, the *afternoon*), months (*January, February*, etc.), seasons (*spring, summer, autumn, winter*), years (*2012, 2016*, etc.).

3 We use .... with days of the week, dates (*4th July*), special days (*my birthday*).

3 **Work in pairs. Ask each other *When ...?* questions.**

> do sports   do your homework   go on holiday
> go to bed   have English classes   school holidays
> wake up   your birthday

When is your birthday?

It's on 13th May.

Vocabulary
Nationalities

1 **Complete the sentences about people from this unit.**

1 Yusra lives in Germany, but she's not ....
2 Yusra is from Syria. She's ....

2 **Complete the table.**

country	nationality	suffix
Australia	Australian	
India	(1)	
(2)	Italian	*-ian* or *-an*
Mexico	(3)	
(4)	Chinese	
Japan	(5)	*-ese*
Portugal	(6)	
Britain	(7)	
Ireland	(8)	
(9)	Spanish	*-ish*
Sweden	(10)	
(11)	French	
Greece	(12)	other

3 **Ask and answer questions about these famous peop**

Where is Alberto Contador from?

He's from Spain. He's Spanish.

Alberto Contador (Spain)

Cristiane Justino (Brazil)

Lionel Messi (Argentina)

Serena Wi (USA)

Writing Part 6

▶ Page 139 Writing bank
Writing Part 6

Work in pairs.

- Which of the sports from the box do you like?
- Which do you want to try?

> badminton   baseball   fishing   golf
> rugby   skiing   surfing

>
> **Exam advice**
> - Include all three points in your email.
> - Write your email in a friendly style.

Work in pairs. Read the exam task. Decide how to follow the instructions.

> Write an email to your English friend, Julie.
> - ask her to go surfing with you at the weekend
> - tell her what to bring
> - say when you want to meet
> Write 25 words or more.

Look at this email to Julie. Complete it with your own ideas.

> i Julie,
>
> o you want to go surfing ....?
> ve got two surfboards, but you should ....
> packed lunch. Let's meet at .... at
> ıy house.
>
> uzy

Now read this task and write your email.

> You want to go horse riding on Sunday with your English friend, Sam.
> Write an email to Sam.
> In your email,
> - ask Sam to go horse riding with you.
> - say where you want to go.
> - tell Sam what to bring.
> Write 25 words or more.

Speaking Part 2

▶ Page 147 Speaking bank
Speaking Part 2

> **Exam advice**
> - In this part, you talk to your partner.
> - The examiner will give you some pictures with a question.
> - Listen carefully to your partner's answers and ask questions.

1 Work in pairs. What sports are in the pictures?

2 Listen to two students. What do they say about each sport? Complete the table with phrases from the box.

> I don't like it.   I don't understand it.   I hate it.
> I like it.   It's boring.   It's exciting, but ...
> I really like it.   It's fun.   I've never tried it.

	boy	girl
tennis		
football		
table tennis		
skiing		
baseball		

3 Work in pairs. Do you like the different sports in the pictures? Say why or why not.

> How often do you play / go ...?

> Who do you play with?

> Which is the best / most exciting / most boring ... ?

It's my favourite sport!   **41**

6 Have you got any homework?

A   B   C   D   E   F   G   H   I

School subjects

1 Work in pairs. Match the words with the pictures.

> art biology chemistry English history
> geography ~~physics~~ maths music

A physics

2 Work in pairs. Do the quiz. Check your answers on page 149.

1 Which is the highest mountain in the world?
2 Which animal has the longest nose?
3 What is the comparative form of *bad*?
4 What is 0.75 x 12?
5 Which falls faster: a melon or a grape?
6 We often put sodium chloride (NaCl) on our food. What is another name for this chemical?
7 When did the First World War end?
8 In which city can you see Leonardo da Vinci's *Mona Lisa*?
9 Which popular musical instrument has six strings?

3 Match the questions from Exercise 2 with the school subjects in the pictures.

4 Which is your favourite school subject? Which is your least favourite? Why?

Listening Part 3

Work in pairs. Answer these questions about your school. Use words from the box to help you.

> a uniform / jeans   famous / modern   funny / kind

1 What do you wear to school?
2 What are your teachers like?
3 What is your school like?

Exam advice

• Read the questions and look carefully at the options.

• If you don't know the answer, you can guess.

Before you listen, read the questions in Exercise 3. What kind of information do you need to listen for?

1 a sport *5*
2 clothing
3 an action
4 a time
5 a topic

For these questions, choose the correct answer. You will hear Louis and Rachel talking about their new schools.

1 What does Louis wear to school?
  A jeans and trainers
  B the school uniform
  C trousers and a T-shirt

2 Lessons at his school start at
  A half past eight
  B a quarter to nine
  C nine o'clock

3 Rachel likes her maths teacher because she
  A speaks quietly
  B makes her laugh
  C is good at explaining things

4 For her English homework, Rachel is going to write about
  A her family
  B a famous actor
  C a sports star

5 What sport is Louis playing at school now?
  A basketball
  B badminton
  C hockey

Listen again and check.

Grammar

have to

▶ **Page 115 Grammar reference**
have to

1 Simon is showing Rachel around his new school. <u>Underline</u> all the examples of *have to* and (*not*) *have to*.

Simon: Welcome to Chester High School, Rachel. Do you live near here?

Rachel: Yes, I can walk to school from my new house.

Simon: Oh, you're lucky. You don't have to get a bus. I live about an hour away, and I have to get up early every morning to catch the bus.

Rachel: I don't like this school uniform very much. Does everyone have to wear it?

Simon: Yes, except when we are doing sports. But in the summer, we don't have to wear a tie. It's too hot.

2 Read the conversation again. Are these statements true (T) or false (F)?

1 It's necessary for Rachel to get a bus to school.
2 It's necessary for Simon to get up early every morning.
3 It's necessary for all students at Chester High School to wear a uniform.
4 It's not necessary for students to wear a tie in the summer.

3 Complete the rules about *have to* with *necessary* or *not necessary*.

Rules

1 We use *have to* and *has to* to talk about things that are ....

2 We use *don't have to* and *doesn't have to* to talk about things that are ....

4 **/p/** /v/ and /f/

Listen and repeat. How do you pronounce *have*? Which one sounds longer?

1 I have two sisters.
2 I have to go to school.
3 We don't have to wear a uniform.

6

5 Work in pairs. Read the rules. Then practise saying the conversation. Then listen and check.

Rules

- We usually say *have* with a /v/ when it means 'to own'.

  I have a new phone!

- But we say /hæf/ in *have to* when we talk about things that are necessary or not necessary.

  I have to work.

A: Have you got any homework?

B: Yes, I have. But I don't have to do it now.

A: When do you have to hand it in?

B: On Thursday.

A: Then you have to do it now because you have a piano lesson on Wednesday evening.

6 What is your school like? Complete the sentences with *have to* or *don't have to*.

1 We _____ wear a uniform.
2 We _____ study English.
3 We _____ do homework every day.
4 We _____ do a test every week.
5 We _____ do sports.
6 We _____ turn off our phones in class.

7 What do you have to do at home? Put the words in order to make questions. Then write true answers.

1 you / have to / Do / meals / cook ?
2 the dishes / you / Do / wash / have to ?
3 clean / Do / have to / your room / you ?
4 have to / go / Do / shopping / you ?
5 someone / wake you up / Does / in the morning / have to ?

Do you have to cook meals?
No, I don't. / Yes, I do.

Vocabulary
Classroom objects

1 Label the picture with words from the box.

> board   desk   dictionary   notebook   pen   pencil
> pencil case   rubber   ruler   textbook   timetable

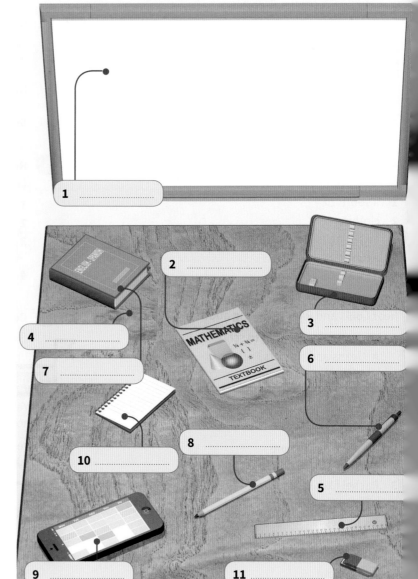

1 ....
2 ....
3 ....
4 ....
5 ....
6 ....
7 ....
8 ....
9 ....
10 ....
11 ....

2 Work in pairs. Ask and answer questions about what you have to bring to school every day.

Do you have to bring a timetable to school every day?

Yes. I have one on my phone.

eading Part 2

- There are three short texts about a similar topic.
- There are seven questions.
- Read the title and look at the pictures first to get an idea of what the texts are about.

Exam advice

Read the article quickly. Match the types of school in each photo with each student.

C

Read the article. For each question, choose the correct answer.

1 Who goes to a school that's in a different country from home?
   A Sara   **B** Marian   **C** Freddy
2 Who learns from only two people?
   A Sara   **B** Marian   **C** Freddy
3 Who has lessons at the weekend?
   A Sara   **B** Marian   **C** Freddy
4 Who has to wear a uniform?
   A Sara   **B** Marian   **C** Freddy
5 Who does well in sports competitions?
   A Sara   **B** Marian   **C** Freddy
6 Who can sometimes decide what to study?
   A Sara   **B** Marian   **C** Freddy
7 Who starts studying at eight in the morning?
   A Sara   **B** Marian   **C** Freddy

Work in pairs. Which kind of school do you think is best?

STUDENT LIFE

SARA

I started going to drama school when I was nine. I love it! It's the biggest drama school in the country. My dad drives me there.

The school day begins with drama lessons at 8 o'clock. In the morning, we do dance, music, theatre, or project work. After lunch, we change into our school uniform and have normal school lessons until 4.30 in the afternoon. At the weekend, we sometimes put on shows, or have sports competitions with other schools.

MARIAN

My parents decided to teach me at home when we moved to the countryside because my old school was too far away.

I get up at 8 o'clock, and begin studying an hour later. In the morning, my dad teaches me maths and science. In the afternoon, I do sports or art with my mum. My weekends are free. I like home schooling because I can choose my own projects, and I can wear what I like.

FREDDY

I live at my school during the term! My parents live in Spain and I go home to see them in the holidays. I often miss them.

We wake up early, at 6.45 in the morning, have breakfast at 8 o'clock, and start the first lesson at 8.45. There are six lessons every weekday. We also have two lessons on Saturday morning. There is no uniform, but we have to wear smart clothes. I'm not great at studying – maths is the hardest for me – but I win a lot of prizes for football and tennis.

6

Grammar
Object pronouns

▶ **Page 115 Grammar reference**
Object pronouns

1 Look at the pictures and answer the questions.

1 Who or what do *her*, *them*, *him* and *it* refer to?

2 Do we use *me*, *you*, *him*, *her*, *it*, *us*, *them* before or after the verb?

He doesn't understand <u>it</u>.
It's too difficult for <u>him</u>.

They love <u>her</u>.
She makes <u>them</u> laugh.

2 Complete the table.

subject pronoun	object pronoun
I	me
it	
you	
we	
he	
she	
they	

3 Complete the sentences with an object pronoun.

1 <u>Geography</u> is my favourite subject, but my sister hates ....*it*.......... .

2 <u>We</u> are unhappy when the teacher gives .... lots of homework.

3 <u>Hala and Sarah</u> are my friends. Let's go and speak to ....

4 <u>Mrs Jones</u> is our head teacher. Everyone likes ....

5 This is my old <u>dictionary</u>. Do you want ....

6 I don't know when <u>your brother's</u> birthday is. Why don't you ask ....

7 Please come here, <u>Monica</u>. I want to talk to ....

8 Help ....! I can't do this exercise.

4 Work in pairs. Write examples of these things. Then ask and answer what you think about the examples.

> a famous man   a famous woman   a music group
> a school subject   a type of food

What do you think about ice cream?

I love it. It's my favourite kind of food.

Vocabulary
Education verbs

1 Read Rachel's blog post. What are her best subjects?

Well, my new school is great. My favourite teacher is Mrs Roberts. She teaches maths. When I leave school I want to go to university and study maths. I'm also learning how to play the violin.

We're taking exams in June. Maths and science exams are easy, but history is more difficult. I'm not very good at it. I never get good marks for my history homework.

2 Choose the correct option.

1 Mrs Roberts *teaches / learns* maths.

2 When did you *learn / study* how to ride a bike?

3 I have to *learn / study* for a test.

4 I hope I *pass / fail* my maths test.

5 We're *taking / learning* lots of exams this summer.

6 She is very clever. She never *passes / fails* tests.

3 Complete the sentences with the correct form of the verbs from the box.

> fail   learn   pass   study   teach

1 I want to .... how to drive a car.

2 Good luck! I hope you .... your test.

3 When Dan leaves school, he wants to .... geography at university.

4 My dad is a teacher. He .... science.

5 I don't want to .... this exam. It's very important that I get over 60%.

4 Work in pairs.

• What musical instrument, language or sport would you like to learn?

• Would you like to go to university?

• What would you like to study?

• How many exams do you take every year?

• What exams do you usually pass?

eading Part 5

• Read the text first to get an idea of what it's about.

• The focus is grammar – you often need to write little words!

Exam advice

In Reading and Writing Part 5, you sometimes need to use a pronoun to complete a text. Complete the sentences with pronouns from the box.

> him   it   my   she   their   you

1   I'm sorry, I forgot to do .... homework!
2   Marco wants you to give .... your phone number.
3   Do you know my sister? I think .... has the same teacher as you.
4   The kids aren't enjoying .... dinner tonight.
5   Lots of people like cheese, but I hate ....
6   Would .... like to come to my party, Emily?

Read the messages quickly. What does Matt want? What does his mother say?

For each question, write the correct answer. Write one word for each gap.

Dad, I have sports after school today and **(0)** ....[........... forgot my trainers. Can you bring **(1)** .... to school for me, please? Mrs Letts, the receptionist, says please leave the trainers **(2)** .... her. Also, I forgot my snack, and I haven't got **(3)** .... money. Can you bring a snack – or some money – as well, please?

Again?! OK, Matt, I'll drive to school. I'll leave **(4)** .... trainers and some money at the reception. **(5)** .... you want those new pencils for your art class? **(6)** .... are on your bed.

Imagine you forget your school bag. Write a text message to one of your parents, asking for help. Ask your partner to check your message.

Speaking Part 2

▶ **Page 147 Speaking bank** Speaking Part 2

• In Part 2, the examiner asks two questions about a topic.

• Each candidate must answer both questions.

• The examiner will also ask a follow-up question (*Why / Why not?*).

Exam advice

1 Complete the table with the school subjects.

> biology   English   chemistry   drama   music   physics

science	arts

2 You will hear an examiner ask Claudia and Jorge these questions. Listen and decide who gives the best answers.

• Do you prefer studying science or arts subjects?
• What's your favourite school subject?

3 Listen again. Complete Claudia's sentences with the linking words from the box.

> and   because   but

1   I prefer the sciences .... I like to learn about the world.
2   I like arts too, ... I don't like studying them.
3   I like biology .... it's interesting, ... I'd like to be a doctor when I'm older.

4 Look at Jorge's answers. Make them better by adding linking words.

1   I don't like science. It's difficult. I like music.
    ....
2   I like my English teacher. She's nice.
    ....

5 Work in pairs. Ask and answer the questions from Exercise 2.

Vocabulary and grammar review

Grammar

1 Complete the sentences with the comparative and superlative forms of the adjectives in brackets.

1 I think my new dress is ......*prettier*...... (pretty) than my old one.

2 Tina swims really well. She's .... (good) swimmer in the school.

3 This is .... (interesting) programme on TV at the moment.

4 Are you .... (happy) than your friends?

5 This book is .... (expensive) than that one.

6 I want to try this dress. It's .... (beautiful) one in the shop!

7 Do you think running is .... (hard) than playing football?

8 This is .... (bad) game on my computer.

2 Complete the blog with *at*, *in* or *on*.

My name is Mason, and I think video games are better than sports. I play them every day!

I usually get up **(1)** ..*at*.. six o'clock **(2)** .... the morning **(3)** .... weekdays, and play on my computer for an hour before breakfast. When I'm at school, I play games on my phone **(4)** .... lunchtime. I like school, but we have to play real sports **(5)** .... Fridays – and I hate that!

When I get home **(6)** .... the afternoon, I go to my room and play more video games. I stop playing **(7)** .... the evening to do my homework. That's usually very easy.

(8) .... the weekend I have lots of time to play. And sometimes **(9)** .... the summer I play all day! My parents don't mind because I do well at school. **(10)** .... my birthday, they never have a problem buying me presents because I'm always happy to get a new video game!

Vocabulary

3 Put the letters in order to make sports.

1 IURGSFN ......*surfing*......
2 TRICKEC ....
3 GOYA ....
4 DOJU ....
5 GLYCCIN ....
6 SCAMTYNGIS ....
7 BOTFLOLA ....
8 STINEN ....
9 SMIGWIMN ....

4 Put the words from Exercise 3 in the correct group.

• You *play*: *cricket*, ... , ...
• You *do*: .... , ... , ...
• You *go*: .... , ... , ...

5 Complete the sentences with the correct nationaliti Use the countries in brackets.

1 Sue isn't English, she's ....*Irish*........ (Ireland).
2 Juan is .... (Mexico).
3 .... (Japan) is a beautiful language.
4 .... (Sweden) people are often good at skiing.
5 I think .... (France) people speak very fa
6 My mother loves .... (Italy) food.
7 .... (Greece) music is really interesting.
8 Grant is .... (Australia).

Grammar

Complete the sentences with the correct form of *have to*.

1 We can't wear jeans to school. We ......*have to*...... wear a uniform.
2 You .... buy any milk today. We've got a lot of it.
3 I'd love to stay out late tonight, but I .... be home before 9 pm.
4 Sam .... do his homework tonight because there's no school tomorrow.
5 Vicky has got a maths test tomorrow, so she .... study this evening.
6 .... (you) go to school on Saturdays?
7 .... (your mother) work every day?

Complete the dialogue with object pronouns.

Lena: There's a great film on TV. Let's watch **(1)** ...*it*... .
Mario: Is Timothée Chalamet in it? I like **(2)** ....
Lena: No, he isn't. Emily Carey is. She's good, too. Do you like **(3)** ....?
Mario: Yes, sure! Or we could watch the music channel. There's a boy band competition on.
Lena: Oh no, not boy bands. I hate **(4)** ....!
Mario: OK, let's go out and walk in the park.
Lena: I don't want to go to the park with **(5)** .... right now, sorry.
Mario: Why don't you want to go with **(6)** ....?
Lena: Because I want to watch this Emily Carey film!

Vocabulary

3 Choose the correct option A, B or C.

1 My mum ......*teaches*...... English to children.
   A teaches   B learns   C studies
2 You have to .... hard at university.
   A teach   B learn   C study
3 I want to .... how to play the piano.
   A teach   B learn   C pass
4 She really wants to .... this exam.
   A pass   B fail   C study
5 I have to .... lots of exams this month.
   A pass   B fail   C take
6 He didn't study. That's why he .... the test.
   A passed   B failed   C took

4 Complete the crossword with words from Unit 6.

Across
3 You have to wear this in some schools.
5 You write things in this.
6 The teacher writes on this at the front of the class.
7 This is the time when you haven't got lessons.

Down
1 You look for words in this book.
2 You use this when you make a mistake in your work.
4 This helps you to draw straight lines.

7 Let's go to the museum

Starting off

1 **Work in pairs.**
- What can you see in the photos?
- Which place do you think is better to live in? Why?

2 **Listen to Ellie and Rory talking about where they live.**
(42)
1 Where do they live?
2 Why do they like it?

3 **Here are some adjectives that Ellie and Rory used. Match each one with its opposite.**

beautiful safe quiet boring

exciting noisy little ugly big dangerous

4 **Work in pairs. What are the good and bad things about where you live?**

My village is a bit boring.

My town is beautiful!

Reading Part 1

- As you read each text, try to decide what situation it appears in.
- Always choose one answer, even if you are not sure it is right.

Exam advic

1 Are there lots of places to go where you live? Make a

2 **Look at this notice. Match the underlined phrases with their definitions.**

1 ....
something that is cheaper
for a limited time

2 ....
costing 50% less

come to the
Wellington Ca
Today's **special of**
half-price coffee
9am-10am.
Lunch 12-2.30

3 **Choose the correct answer.**

A The café is only open between 9 am and 10 am too
B The menu has cheap meals before 12 o'clock.
C There is a time when you can get cheaper coffee.

For each question, choose the correct answer.

Em,
My class finished late, so I missed the 7.30 bus. Let's meet at the bus station at 8.30. We can catch the 8.40 bus.
Lara

A Lara is explaining why she couldn't catch the 7.30 bus.
B Lara wants Em to get the 8.30 bus.
C Lara is letting Em know that the last bus is at 8.40.

Rachel,
...m bought our tickets online for the museum exhibition.
...n you give me the money in class tomorrow?
...ey're £10. Thanks, Jo

What should Rachel do?
A Send an email to Jo's mum.
B Check the museum website for tickets.
C Take some money to school tomorrow.

...o,
...hope you're feeling better now. Our history homework is
...o write about a famous building that you like. Bring it to
...he next class. Zhang

Why did Zhang send this message?
A He wants to know what Jo is writing about.
B He wants to tell Jo about the homework.
C He wants to know why Jo missed class.

Hospital visiting 2–4 pm
Two visitors per bed and no children under 7.

A Children under seven can visit if they come with an adult.
B No visitors can come into the hospital before 4 pm.
C It's not possible for three or more people to visit at the same time.

Science Museum Trip
...students interested in next Wednesday's trip must give their
...es to Mr Smith before Friday. Only five seats left on the bus!

A If you want to go on the trip, tell Mr Smith soon.
B The museum is not open on Friday.
C Only science students can go on the trip.

Grammar
Past simple

▶ **Page 116 Grammar reference:**
Past simple

1 **Read Sandra's blog. Where does she live now? Does she enjoy living there?**

Here are two of my favourite photos.

I <u>liked</u> living in our little village in Spain, so when my parents (got) new jobs in Australia, I felt sad. All my friends were in the village, and I didn't want to leave them. I didn't know anybody in Sydney!

Last year we left our old home and got on a plane to a new life in a new country.

How did I feel about that? I hated it at first. My new school was much bigger than my old one, and I felt very small and alone. I didn't speak much English, so it was

difficult to make new friends. I wanted to go back to our village.

But slowly I began to feel happier. My parents gave me a camera for my birthday. Then I joined the school photography club and I met some interesting people. Last month, there was a competition called 'Pictures of the City' and I decided to enter it. I won a prize, and they showed my photograph in the city library.

I love living here now. It's a beautiful place, and much more exciting than my old village.

2 **Number these events in the order they happen.**
a Sandra joined a photography club.
b Sandra left Spain and moved to Australia.
c Sandra won a photography competition.
d Her parents found new jobs.
e Sandra lived in a village. 1
f Her parents gave her a camera.
g Sandra started her new school.

3 **Read the blog and the sentences from Exercise 2 again.**
<u>Underline</u> all the regular past simple verbs.
(Circle) all the irregular verbs, and *was* and *were*.

4 **Look at the blog again and find an example of a past simple question and a negative.**

5 Complete the rules with words from the box.

> adding -ed or -d   did   didn't   finished   was and were

1 We use the past simple to talk about actions that happened in the past and are now ....
2 We can make regular past forms by ....
3 We use .... before a verb to make questions in the past.
4 We use .... before a verb to make negatives in the past.
5 .... are the past of *is* and *are*. We don't use them with *did* to make questions or negative sentences.

6 Exam candidates often make mistakes with past simple forms. Correct the mistakes in each of these sentences.

1 Last night, I ~~go~~ to a disco on the beach. *went*
2 On my last holiday, I went to Miami and I stayied at a five-star hotel.
3 Did you played volleyball and hockey at the lake?
4 The T-shirt costed me £25.
5 He maked her a sandwich.
6 Yesterday, I have watched a tennis competition.

7 Complete the conversation with the past simple form of the verbs in brackets.

Tom: Hi, Sandra. I **(1)** ....*saw*.......... (see) your photo in the library. It's fantastic.
Sandra: Thanks, Tom. I **(2)** .... (take) it on New Year's Eve, when I **(3)** .... (go) into the city with my family.
Tom: What time **(4)** .... (be) it?
Sandra: It was just after midnight. The fireworks **(5)** .... (be) beautiful, so I **(6)** .... (decide) to take lots of photos.
Tom: How many photos **(7)** .... (you / take)?
Sandra: Hundreds! But most of them **(8)** .... (not be) very good.
Tom: **(9)** .... (be / you) surprised when you won the photo competition?
Sandra: Yes, I was! I **(10)** .... (know) it was a good photo, but I **(11)** .... (not think) it was good enough to win a prize.
Tom: **(12)** .... (you / have) a party?
Sandra: No, I didn't. But my parents **(13)** .... (buy) me a smartphone.

8 Work in pairs. Choose the correct option in *italics*. Ask and answer the questions.

1 What time *did / were* you go to bed last night?
2 *Did / Were* you at school yesterday afternoon?
3 What *did / were* you have for breakfast this morning?
4 *Did / Were* you go on holiday last year?
5 *Did / Was* the weather nice yesterday?
6 How *did / were* you get to school this morning?
7 *Did / Was* your last homework easy?
8 Where *did / were* you at 8 o'clock last night?

9 **/ P /** past simple -ed endings
43 There are three ways to pronounce -ed endings: /d/, /t/ and /ɪd/. Listen and repeat the verbs.

/d/	/t/	/ɪd/
showed	finished	started

10 Listen and complete the table with the <u>underlined</u>
44 verbs.

She <u>lived</u> in a village. She <u>liked</u> it. She <u>wanted</u> to stay the

11 Listen and repeat. Then add the words to the table.
45

> asked   arrived   joined   waited   worked   visite

12 Use the ideas below to write five questions.

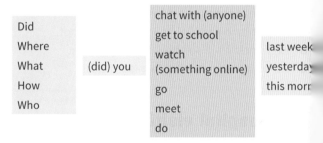

Did		chat with (anyone)	
Where		get to school	last week
What	(did) you	watch	yesterday
How		(something online)	this morr
Who		go	
		meet	
		do	

Did you chat with anyone yesterday?

Yes, I did. I chatted with my frie

13 Work in pairs. Ask and answer your questions. Be careful with the pronunciation of the verbs!

Vocabulary
Buildings

Label the photos with words from the box.

~~church~~ cinema factory hospital hotel
mosque museum post office stadium train station

....

2 .... *church* ....

....

4 ....

....

6 ....

....

8 ....

....

10 ....

2 Have you got any of these buildings where you live? Have you got more than one?

Listening Part 4

Exam advice
• Read the questions carefully and underline the key words.
• Check your answers on the second listening.

1 Work in pairs. Tell your partner about a nice place you visited recently. What did you see? Did you enjoy it?

2 **46** Listen. For these questions, choose the correct answer.

1 You will hear two friends talking about a place they visited. What did they think of it?
A It was expensive.
B It was small.
C It was boring.

2 You will hear a teacher talking to her class about a trip. Where did they go?
A a restaurant
B a factory
C a house

3 You will hear two friends talking about their town. Why do they both like it?
A It's full of interesting people.
B It has a great sports stadium.
C It's close to the sea.

4 You will hear a father asking his daughter about what she did last night. What did she do?
A She went to the cinema.
B She went online.
C She went to a restaurant.

5 You will hear a boy leaving a message for his friend. Where does he want to meet?
A the stadium
B the post office
C the supermarket

3 **46** Listen again and check.

Grammar
Imperatives

▶ **Page 117 Grammar reference**
Imperatives

1 <u>Underline</u> the verbs in the sentence.

Meet me at the main entrance. Don't be late!

Rules

1 To tell somebody to do something, we use the infinitive without *to*.

2 To tell somebody not to do something, we use *not* + the infinitive without *to*.

2 Read the commands. Then listen and match them with the sounds (1–7).
47

a   Be quiet!
b   Don't cry.
c   Answer the phone. 1
d   Give it some milk.
e   Wake up.
f   Don't laugh.
g   Don't jump on the bed!

3 Work in pairs. Imagine a visitor is coming to your town. Tell them what to do and what not to do. Use verbs from the box.

eat   go   see   visit

Visit the castle. It's beautiful.
Don't go to expensive restaurants.

Vocabulary
Directions

1 Match the <u>underlined</u> words with the symbols on the map.

1   Turn left at the <u>traffic lights</u>. A
2   Go over the <u>crossing</u>.
3   Turn right at the <u>roundabout</u>.
4   Cross the <u>bridge</u>.
5   The <u>square</u> is on the right.

2 Where does this person want to go from the station? Read the directions, look at the map, and complete the question.

1   **A:** Excuse me, where is the .... ?
    B: Turn left out of the station. Go straight over the roundabout, then turn left at the traffic lights. It on Barnley Street.

2   **A:** Excuse me, where is the .... ?
    B: Come out of the station and go over the crossing. Then turn right. It's on the left.

3   **A:** Excuse me, can you tell me where the .... is, please?
    B: Yes, turn left out of the station then take the firs turning on the left. It's on the right.

3 Work in pairs. Imagine you are a tourist in the square. Take turns to ask for and give directions to other pla on the map.

Excuse me, where is the cinema?

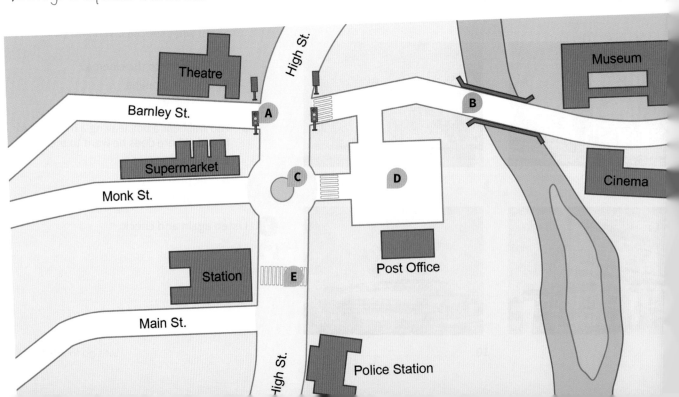

Speaking Part 2

▶ **Page 147 Speaking bank**
Speaking Part 2

> • Be prepared to give reasons for any answers you give.
>
> **Exam advice**

Listen to the conversation. What places in the pictures do the students mention?

Listen again and complete the sentences with *The reason* **or** *because.*

1   I don't like shopping centres .... I don't like shopping.

2   .... I love them is that I often meet my friends there.

3   I don't go to the stadium .... I'm not really interested in sport.

---

3 **Rewrite the sentences using** *because* **or** *The reason.*

1   I like going to museums because I'm interested in history.

The reason I like going to museums is that I'm interested in history.

2   The reason I hate the beach is that I don't like sand.
I hate ....

3   I don't like museums because they're boring.
The ....

4 **Talk to your partner about the different places in Exercise 1. Say why you like or don't like them.**

> I like going to the beach.
>
> Why?
>
> The reason I like going there is …

Writing Part 6

▶ **Page 139 Writing bank**
Writing Part 6

1 **Read the message quickly. Which questions does Jenny answer?**

1   Where did you go?

2   Why did you go there?

3   Who did you go with?

4   Did you like it?

5   How often do you go there?

> Hi Sandra,
> Yesterday I go to the car museum in town.
> My friend Julie were with me. I didn't liked it because I think cars are boring!
> Jenny

2 **Read the message again and <u>underline</u> any mistakes.**

3 **Rewrite the message without the mistakes.**

> • When you have finished your writing, always check it for mistakes.
>
> **Exam advice**

4 **Do the task.**

> You went to an interesting place in town yesterday. Write an email to your English friend, Jo.
> In your email:
> • tell Jo **where** you went
> • say **who** you went with
> • say **why** you liked or didn't like it.

8 Did you get my message?

Are you **crazy** about the **internet?**

Starting off

1 Work in pairs. Do the quiz.

1 How much time do you spend on the internet?

A less than 10 hours a week
B between 10 and 30 hours a week
C more than 30 hours a week

2 You want to have a party. How do you invite your friends?

A You speak to them.
B You send invitations by post.
C You email, text, or message them.

3 What makes you most excited?
A Your favourite band is coming to town.
B There's a new computer game you want to try.
C Your favourite celebrity likes one of your social media posts.

4 Do you know how many friends and followers you've got on social media?

A I don't use social media.
B Yes, more or less.
C Yes, I know exactly how many!

5 How often do you upload photos of your food to social media?

A never
B sometimes
C every day

6 What is the most important thing to take with you on a long journey?

A a book to read
B a film to watch
C your smartphone

7 You want to learn how to do something difficul What do you do?

A Ask somebody to teach you.
B Look in a book.
C Watch a video online.

8 A friend invites you to their house for the first time. What's your first question?

A How far away is it?
B Have you got any computer games?
C Have you got wi-fi?

2 Now check your score on page 149. Do you agree wi the results? Compare your score with your partner's

Listening Part 5

- Always cross out the example answer in the second column so you don't choose it by mistake.

- You will often hear two things mentioned for one question. Only one of them is correct. Listen carefully to decide which one to choose.

Exam advice

Look at the advertisement. What is a computer fair?

COMPUTER FAIR
Saturday 10 am – 5 pm
@Hollyrood Sports Centre
Laptops, smartphones, cameras, memory cards, keyboards, computer games, AND MORE!
All at discount prices!

Match the words from the advertisement with the photos. Which object is in the picture but not in the advertisement? What is it called?

3 For these questions, choose the correct answer. You will hear Marta talking to her dad about what she and her friends bought at the computer fair. Write two things (A–H) that are mentioned for each person.

People		Objects	
Marta	....C....	**A**	camera
1 Ollie	....E.... and	**B**	case
2 Susie	.... and	**C**	computer game
3 Anna	.... and	**D**	keyboard
4 Pedro	.... and	**E**	laptop
5 Miguel	.... and	**F**	memory card
		G	mouse
		H	smartphone

4 Listen again. What did each person actually buy? Choose the correct option from the two in Exercise 2.

Vocabulary
Technology verbs

1 Work in pairs. Look at the technology facts below. Do you think they are true for you?

Teenagers and technology

- Teenagers **check** their social media messages up to 100 times per day.
- 95% of teenagers **upload** selfies to social media.
- Most teenagers **download** music and films from the internet.
- Teenagers don't **email** each other very often.
- A typical teenager **sends** messages about 15 times per day.

2 Complete the sentences with the correct form of a word in bold from Exercise 1.

1 I don't ....email........ my friends very often because it's easier to use social media messaging.
2 My friend .... films from the internet, because it's cheaper than going to the cinema.
3 When I want to contact someone, I ....them a message.
4 I .... two new selfies yesterday.
5 My sister .... her social media page about 30 times yesterday.

3 Work in pairs. Are the sentences in Exercise 2 true for you?

Did you get my message? 57

8

Grammar
Past continuous

▶ **Page 119 Grammar reference**
Past continuous

1 Work in pairs. Do you know any videos that went viral?

> *viral* adjective (INTERNET)
> used to describe something that quickly becomes very popular or well known by being published on the internet
> *The video went **viral** and after a few days millions of people saw it.*

2 Read Joshua's blog. Where was he when he got the surprising news?

100,029 views

Last month was my little sister Meg's birthday, and we were having a party for her in the garden. Music was playing, and Meg was walking around eating a biscuit. Suddenly a new song came on the radio. At that moment, Meg stopped, dropped her biscuit, and danced! She loved that song!

Everybody was watching her. While she was dancing, I was recording her on my phone.

That night, I uploaded the video to the internet and went to bed. I was sleeping when my phone rang at 7 o'clock the next morning.

'Hi Dan, it's Marco. I saw your funny video of Meg. Do you know it's got 100,000 views already?'

My baby sister was a viral video star!

3 Underline the verbs in each sentence below. Then answer the questions.

- Music was playing and Meg was walking around.
- Meg stopped, dropped her biscuit, and danced.

1 Which sentence describes two actions happening at the same time?
2 Which sentence describes one action happening after another?

4 Look at the timeline. Did Meg start walking before or after the song came on the radio?

> a song came on the radio.
> _____
> Meg was walking …

5 Underline the verbs below. Which action started first?

I was sleeping when my phone rang.

6 Choose the correct words to complete the rules.

Rules

1 We use the past *simple / continuous* to say what was happening at a particular time in the past.
2 We use the past *simple / continuous* to talk about two or more actions happening at the same time in the past.
3 We use the past simple and continuous together to talk about an action that happened *in the middle of / after* another action.

7 Complete the sentences with the past continuous or past simple form of the verbs.

1 The sun ..*was shining*.. (shine) and we ..*were having*.. (have) lunch in the garden.
2 I .... (text) you after I .... (wake up).
3 The baby .... (sleep) in her room at 1 o'clock.
4 It .... (not rain) yesterday, so we .... (go) to the park in the afternoon.
5 When Danie's mother .... (come) home, he .... (watch) TV.
6 At 8 o'clock last night I .... (read) a book.
7 What .... (you / do) at 7 o'clock this morning?

8 Write the questions.

1 What / you / do / at 9 o'clock last night?
2 What / you / do / at 1 o'clock yesterday afternoon?
3 What / your parents / do / at 8 o'clock last night?
4 What / you / do / ten minutes ago?
5 you / sleep / at 11 o'clock last night?
6 you / do / your homework / at 7 o'clock last night?

What were you doing at 9 o'clock last night?

9 Work in pairs. First, guess what your partner was doing at the times from Exercise 8. Then find out.

> Were you sleeping at 11 o'clock last night?

> No, I wasn't. I was listening to music.

Reading Part 2

* Read all the texts and when you find the text that has the answer to the question, underline the part where the answer is.

Do you watch videos online? Who is your favourite video maker? Do you ever make your own videos, or know someone who does?

Quickly read the texts about the three video makers. Match them with the topics from the box.

> animals   daily life   games

Read the questions. Then read Davina's text carefully. Which questions are about Davina? Underline the parts of the text which show the answers.

Read Sonja and Joana's texts and choose the correct answer.

	Davina	Sonja	Joana
Who makes videos which are funny?	A	B	C
Who began making videos a year ago?	A	B	C
Who shares something they can do?	A	B	C
Who likes people to ask questions?	A	B	C
Who receives good wishes on special days?	A	B	C
Who posts more than one video a week?	A	B	C
Who earns money from her videos?	A	B	C

Vocabulary

Music

1 Listen and match the music you hear with the playlist.

Genre	...	
1 classical		
2 jazz	5	R&B
3 opera	6	rock
4 pop	7	electronic/dance

2 What other genres of music do you know? Can you think of examples of bands or singers for each kind of music?

3 Work in small groups.

1 Do you listen to a lot of music?
2 What music do you like?
3 How often do you listen to it?
4 How do you listen to it?

4 What is the most popular kind of music in your group? Tell the class.

THREE VIDEO MAKERS

DAVINA

I started my video channel twelve months ago because I wanted to show the world the animals on our farm. Then I began to collect other animal videos and put them together into one long video. I upload one of those every month. They're good fun to make. The animals in them are from all around the world. The cat videos are the favourites! Some of my followers are very kind. On my birthday I get lots of nice messages – and sometimes poems!

JOANA

Computer games are more popular than Hollywood movies, and every week I make a video of myself playing one of them. I'm really good, so millions of people watch me to learn how to do it. In fact, games companies pay me to make the videos – it's good advertising for them. Game players sometimes have a problem and can't get to the next level. They just need to ask me, and I can show them what to do. It makes me feel good to help them.

SONJA

...ople enjoy watching my videos. I've got ...ousands of followers. I could make money from ...vertisements, but I decided not to do that. My ...st video was about what I do when I get home ...om school, including doing my homework. ...at doesn't sound very exciting, but the way I ...alk about it makes people laugh – that's why I'm popular. I usually ...pload a video every three days. I wish I could do it more often!

8

Grammar
can/can't, could/couldn't

▶ **Page 120 Grammar reference:**
can/can't, could/couldn't

1 Do you think our lives are easier than our parents' lives because of technology? Why? / Why not?

2 Match sentences 1–8 with photos A–H.

1 You couldn't find information very quickly.
2 You can carry thousands of songs with you.
3 You couldn't put a telephone in your pocket.
4 You could easily get lost in a strange place.
5 You can find information very quickly. F
6 You couldn't carry thousands of songs with you.
7 You can put a phone in your pocket.
8 You can't easily get lost in a strange city.

3 Complete the rules with *present* or *past*.

Rules

1 We use *can* and *can't* to talk about ability in the
....

2 We use *could* and *couldn't* to talk about ability in the
....

3 We use the infinitive without *to* / *-ing form* after all forms of *can* and *could*.

4 Exam candidates often make mistakes with modals like *can/can't* and *could/couldn't*. Correct the mistake in each sentence.

1 She opened her bag, but she couldn't ~~to~~ find her mobile phone.
2 I can playing games on my phone.
3 I couldn't listened to music on my old phone.
4 You can't getting the bus – it's too late.
5 She could used a computer when she was three.
6 Sorry, I can't helping you.

5 **/p/** *can* /*can't*

Listen and repeat. Notice how *can* /*can't* are pronounced.

1 My phone can do lots of things.
2 Can it take photos?
3 Yes, it can.
4 But it can't do my homework.

6 Match the sounds (a–c) with the rules (1–3).

a /kɑːnt/   **b** /kən/   **c** /kæn/

1 In positive sentences and questions, *can* is pronounced ../kən/.. .
2 In positive short answers, it is pronounced ....
3 In negative sentences, *can't* is pronounced ....

7 Work in pairs. What things can you do now that you couldn't do when you were four years old?

> draw   play an instrument   ride a bike
> use a smartphone   swim   write my name

Can you ride a bike?

Yes, I can.

Could you ride a bike when you were four?

No, I couldn't.

Reading Part 5

1 Complete each sentence with a word from the table.

articles	pronouns	verbs
the	me	were
an	him/her	have
a	they	do
prepositions	**quantifiers**	**modals**
on	many	can/can't
in	few	could/couldn't
off	some	must

1 Dad went to ....the.......... bank. (article)
2 They .... sleeping at 10 o'clock last night. (verb)
3 Turn that TV .... and do your homework! (preposition)
4 There weren't .... people at the party. (quantifier)
5 Can you help ....? I can't do this on my own. (pronoun)
6 Would you like ....cup of tea? (article)
7 .... you help me, please? (modal)

Work in pairs. Read the email. Decide what type of word you need to complete each space.

- Look closely at each sentence and decide what kind of word goes in each space (e.g. a verb, a pronoun, etc.).
- Check the tense that each sentence needs to use.

Exam advice

Complete the email. Write one word in each gap.

Sam,

his morning I **(0)** ....was.......... downloading some music to
y phone in my room when **(1)** .... internet stopped
mpletely! I tried to fix it, but I couldn't. **(2)** .... I come to
ur house and use your wi-fi, please?

n trying to download the new song by our favourite band, The
ue Days. **(3)** .... you know it? It was **(4)** ....
e radio yesterday. The DJ announced the band's tour dates.
n really excited! They're coming in July and I really want to see
) ....! Let's hope the tickets don't cost too
) .... or I won't be able to go.

chelle

Speaking Part 1

▶ **Page 146 Speaking bank**
Speaking Part 1

1 Listen to an examiner speaking to two candidates. Complete the examiner's questions.

1 Tell me about your ....computer.... or ....?
2 What do you .... it for?
3 Do you like .... games?
4 What kind of .... do you like?
5 .... do you listen to music?
6 Tell me something about the last piece of music you .... to.
7 What .... the song about?

2 Which two questions are in the past tense?

- Listen carefully to the examiner's question and answer it in the same tense.
- Don't worry if the examiner stops you.

Exam advice

3 Work in pairs. Discuss the questions from Exercise 1. Ask follow-up questions (e.g *Why / Why not?*).

The Blue Days

7 Vocabulary and grammar review

Grammar

1 Complete the sentences with the past simple form of the verbs in the box.

> not like   meet   not win   begin   ~~join~~
> not feel   give   drink   not go

1 I ......*joined*...... the dance club last week.
2 We .... a lot of nice people at the party.
3 Jon .... me a football for my birthday.
4 Sondra .... well yesterday, so she .... to school.
5 The children .... the film – it was boring.
6 I .... all the water in the bottle.
7 Dan was sad because he .... the race.
8 It .... to rain just after two o'clock.

2 Write the questions for the answers.

1 *What did you buy?* ....
   I bought a magazine.
2 ....?
   No, they didn't enjoy the party.
3 ....?
   She went to the cinema.
4 ....?
   Yes, it rained yesterday.
5 ....?
   I laughed because it was funny.
6 ....?
   I spoke to my teacher.
7 ....?
   They got there by bus.
8 ....?
   No, I wasn't late.

3 Complete the sentences with an imperative verb.

1 Don't watch that. ......*Watch*...... this! It's much better.
2 Write in your notebook. .... in your textbook!
3 .... fast. Walk slowly.
4 .... to me. Don't listen to him.
5 Call me now. .... me later.
6 Don't eat the cake now. .... a sandwich first.
7 .... to the cinema. Go to the museum.

Vocabulary

4 Complete the words to make names of buildings and places.

1 c i n e m a
2 b _ _ _ ge
3 m _ _ q _ _
4 _ _ ct _ _ y
5 ch _ _ _ _
6 h _ _ _ l
7 r _ _ n _ a _ _ ut
8 _ _ sp _ _ _ l
9 s _ _ _ re
10 s _ _ d _ _ m

5 Complete the sentences with words from Exercise 4.

1 We visited our uncle in ......*hospital*...... when he was i
2 My dad is an engineer in a car ....
3 There is a big .... over the river in my tow
4 82,000 people can sit in the football club's new ....
5 I didn't enjoy the film because the .... wa full of noisy children.
6 My parents stayed in a .... on a beach wh they went on holiday.

6 Complete the directions with words from the box.

> ~~turn~~   on   traffic   straight   take
> second   over   turn

A: Excuse me. Where is the hospital?
B: (1) ......*Turn*...... left out of the bus station.
Go **(2)** .... over the roundabout, then **(3)** .... right into Green Street.
(4) .... the first turning on the right and it's on your left.
A: Can you tell me where the supermarket is, please?
B: Yes. Go down this road. Go **(5)** .... the br and go straight **(6)** .... for about 200 me
Turn left at the **(7)** .... lights and take th **(8)** .... turning on the left.

Grammar

Match the beginning of each sentence (1–6) with its ending (a–f).

1 We were lying in the garden   f
2 Someone took my bike
3 My brother hurt his leg
4 When I saw Emily in town
5 The children were sleeping on the sofa
6 You weren't listening to the teacher

a she was talking to Jenny.
b when he was playing hockey.
c when she told us about the test.
d when I was studying in the library.
e when their parents came home.
f when it started to rain.

Complete the sentences with the past continuous of the verb in brackets.

1 I ....*was messaging*............ (message) my best friend in the English lesson.
2 What .... (you / do) when I phoned you yesterday?
3 It... (not rain) when she left the house, but it is now.
4 .... (your parents / sleep) when you got home?
5 Dan and Ellie .... (have) dinner at 7.30 last night.
6 You .... (not watch) that terrible film, were you?

Complete the conversation with *can, can't, could* or *couldn't* and the verb in brackets.

Jill: Hi, Adam, is that a new app that you're using?
Adam: Yes, it's great. It (1) ....*can do*........ (do) lots of things that I (2) .... (not do) before.
Jill: Like what? What (3) .... (you / use) it for?
Adam: When I'm running, it (4) .... (show) me how far I'm running. And it (5) .... (tell) me how fast I'm going, too.
Jill: I had an app that (6) .... (do) that, but I deleted it!
Adam: Why?

Jill: Because it always posted my information online, so everyone (7) .... (see) how much I was running. I didn't like that.
Adam: OK, my app has that, too, but I (8) .... (switch) if off, so people (9) .... (see) my private information. Only I (10) ....!

Vocabulary

4 **Complete the note with the verbs from the box.**

> check   download   email   upload   send

> I love technology. The most important thing in my bedroom isn't my bed – it's my tablet !
> I use it every day to (1) .... things online and to (2) .... films or music. My parents use their computers to (3) .... their friends, but I don't do that very much. I (4) .... messages to my friends about 50 times a day on my phone or on social media. I often (5) ....photos, too, so other people can see what I'm doing.

5 **Put the letters in order to make different kinds of music.**

1 SCALCALIS   ......*classical*......
2 OPP   ....
3 ARP   ....
4 PAREO   ....
5 KORC   ....
6 ZAJZ   ....

9 I love that film!

WHAT'S HAPPENING?

Your guide to the best places to go in town.

The Art of the Camera

Beautiful exhibition from some of the best young (1) .... working today.

Richmond Hall, 4–6 August

FREE!

Winning Voices

More than 20 (2) .... play their best songs in a competition to win a great prize: a place in the national final and the chance to make their own album.

Monterey Student Centre, 6 o'clock

Tickets £7.50 – £10

Film Club

Tonight's movie at the Young People's Film Club is the classic Toy Story. It stars (3) .... Tim Allen as the voice of Buzz Lightyear.

Starts 6.30. Tickets £2

Streetlife Dance Group

Come and see the amazing 'SDG' at the Atlas Centre. Twenty-four (4) .... aged between 11 and 18 show off their skills for you.

Starting 7 pm. Tickets £15.00

Theatre Royale

The final performance of Just you, me and Bobby is tonight. This is your last chance to watch this wonderful (5) .... Don't miss it!

8 pm. Tickets £9, £7 and £5.50

Starting off

1 Work in pairs. Look at the guide.

   1 Which of the things would you like to go to?

   2 What kind of things can you do where you live?

2 Complete the guide with words from the box.

> actor   bands   dancers   photographers   play

Reading Part 4

1 What is your favourite film? How many times have you seen it?

2 Work in pairs. Look at these famous bears.

- Which do you know?
- What do you know about them?
- Do you know any of their stories?

> **Exam advice**
> - Always read the whole text before you try to answer the questions.
> - Look carefully at the words around the space, and make sure that your answer goes with them.
> - Try to think of a word which fits in the gap before you look at the options.

3 For each question, choose the correct answer for each gap.

Michael Bond

Paddington's Adventures

Illustrated by Peggy Fortnum

Paddington Bear

One day, over 60 years ago, an English writer called Michael Bond went into a London shop to buy a present for his wife. There he **(1)** .... a small toy bear, sitting by himself, the last one **(2)** .... on the shelf. He brought the bear home and, because they lived near Paddington train station, he **(3)** .... to call him Paddington.

Later, Michael wrote a story about Paddington Bear, which became a book. That book **(4)** .... Michael Bond and his funny little bear very famous all over the world. Now there are very popular new films about the adventures of Paddington – and it isn't **(5)** .... children who enjoy them. Paddington is lots of people's **(6)** .... bear, young and old.

1	**A**	watched	**B**	saw	**C**	looked
2	**A**	went	**B**	stayed	**C**	left
3	**A**	decided	**B**	thought	**C**	took
4	**A**	did	**B**	made	**C**	pushed
5	**A**	only	**B**	alone	**C**	first
6	**A**	attractive	**B**	favourite	**C**	excellent

4 Do you like stories about animals? What are your favourite ones?

9

Grammar

Verbs with -ing or to infinitive

▶ **Page 121 Grammar reference**
-ing or *to* infinitive

1 Look at the picture. Who is it? What is she doing?

2 Listen and complete the interview with a clown.

53

> being   doing   making   talking   ~~to become~~
> to do   to laugh   to learn   to work

David: Why did you decide **(1)** ....to become.... a clown?

Tanya: Well, I love **(2)** .... – everybody does, don't they? When I was 11, my parents got a clown to come to my birthday party. He was very funny, and I thought, 'I want **(3)** .... that,' so I did!

David: Is it difficult **(4)** .... to be a clown?

Tanya: Juggling is the hardest thing. That took months of practice!

David: What's the best thing about **(5)** .... a clown?

Tanya: That's easy – I love **(6)** .... people laugh.

David: Do you make much money?

Tanya: No, not much! I do children's parties for free. It's just something I enjoy **(7)** ....

David: What about the future?

Tanya: I'd like **(8)** .... in the film industry when I finish school.

David: Well, good luck, and thanks for **(9)** .... to me.

Tanya: Thanks. It was fun.

3 Find examples of these rules in the interview.

> **Rules**
>
> 1 Some verbs are followed by the *to* infinitive.
> *Decide to become*
> 2 Some verbs are followed by the *-ing* form. ....
> 3 When a verb follows a preposition (except *to*), it is always an *-ing* form. ....
> 4 *Would like* is followed by the *to* infinitive. ....
> 5 When a verb follows an adjective, it is usually a *to* infinitive. ....
> 6 Some verbs can be followed by either the *to* infinitive or the *-ing* form. ....

4 Complete the sentences with the correct form of the verb in brackets.

1 Do you want ....to go........ (go) to the rock concert
2 We enjoy .... (work) with young people.
3 I'd like .... (help) you, but I'm very busy.
4 Don't worry about .... (clean) your room I'll do it for you.
5 He doesn't mind .... (sleep) on the sofa.
6 What job do you hope .... (do) when you leave school?
7 Thank you for .... (come) to my party.
8 I finished .... (read) at 12 o'clock.
9 Dad promised .... (buy) me a camera.
10 I'm tired of .... (wait) for my friend.

5 /P/ *-ing* forms

54

Underline all the verbs in Exercise 4 ending in *-ing*. How are they pronounced? Listen and check.

6 Write four true and one false sentence about yourself

Write about something you:
- hate doing
- are good at doing
- hope to do in the future
- worry about doing
- are learning to do

7 Work in pairs. Read your sentences to your partner. Can your partner guess which sentence is false?

8 Exam candidates often make mistakes with infinitive and *-ing* forms. Correct the mistake in each sentence

1 I don't like ~~cook~~. *cooking*
2 Thank you for to send letter to me.
3 I'd like know what you had for dinner last night.
4 I want invited you to my house.
5 It soon stopped to rain.

ocabulary

uggesting, accepting and refusing

Match the words with the definitions.

1 suggest   **2** accept   **3** refuse

a to agree to something
b to say an idea or a plan for someone to think about
c to say that you will not do something

Work in pairs. Read the conversation. How many suggestions does Carl make?

Carl: There's a good film on TV tonight. <u>Why don't we</u> stay at home and watch it?
Emma: <u>No, thanks.</u> I'd like to go out.
Carl: OK. <u>How about</u> going to the theatre?
Emma: <u>I'd rather not.</u> Some plays are difficult to understand.
Carl: OK. <u>Shall we</u> go to the Atlas Centre? The Streetlife Dance Group are doing a show tonight.
Emma: <u>Good idea.</u> How much are the tickets?
Carl: About £15 each.
Emma: Oh dear. That's a lot.
Carl: Do you still want to go?
Emma: <u>I don't think so.</u>
Carl: OK. <u>Would you like to</u> go to the school concert?
Emma: <u>Yeah, sure.</u> Good idea.

Complete the table with the <u>underlined</u> phrases from Exercise 1.

suggesting (?)	accepting ✓	refusing ✗
Why don't we		

4   **Work in pairs. Do the task.**

- **Student A:** You want to go out with Student B this evening. Make three suggestions.
- **Student B:** Refuse the first two suggestions and accept the last one.

> Shall we go to the Film Club tonight?

> I'd rather not …

Listening Part 2

- Look carefully at the form and think about what type of answers you will have to write.
- You will often hear two or more possible answers for each gap, but only one is correct.

Exam advice

1   **Look at the poster for a music concert. Think of things that you need to know about it.**

Where is the concert?

2   **For these questions, write the correct answer in each gap. You will hear some information about a concert. Write one word or a number or a date or a time.**

55

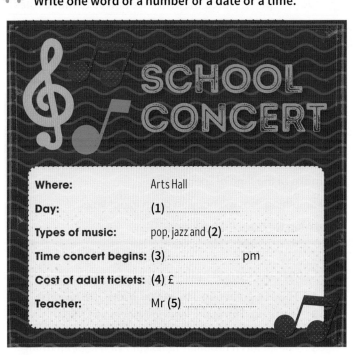

SCHOOL CONCERT

Where:	Arts Hall
Day:	(1) ....
Types of music:	pop, jazz and (2) ....
Time concert begins:	(3) .... pm
Cost of adult tickets:	(4) £ ....
Teacher:	Mr (5) ....

9

Grammar

The future with the present simple, present continuous and *will*

▶ **Page 122 Grammar reference**
The future

1 Francesca has two tickets for a band competition. Read her conversation with Daniel. Does he want to go with her?

Francesca: Hey, Daniel. They're having a band competition at Rock City tonight. It starts at 6 o'clock. Do you want to come?

Daniel: I don't know. It'll probably be boring.

Francesca: It won't be boring at all! Come on. It finishes at 10.

Daniel: OK. Let's go. I'll get my coat.

Francesca: Great! I'll ask my dad to take us. The Jacks are playing first, and I don't want to miss them.

2 Read the conversation again.

• Circle two examples of the present continuous to talk about the future.

• Underline two examples of the present simple to talk about the future.

• Underline and circle two examples of *will* to talk about the future.

3 Work in pairs. Match the sentence halves to make rules.

Rules

1 The present continuous can be used to talk about

2 The future with *will* can be used to talk about

3 The present simple can be used to talk about

a what we think will happen in the future, or decisions we make at the time of speaking.

b something that will happen at an exact time.

c a plan we have for the future.

4 Choose the correct options.

1 This is a great film. I think you *'ll love / 're loving* it.

2 Hurry up. The plane *leaving / leaves* at 12.30 this afternoon.

3 The children probably *don't eat / won't eat* anything tonight because they're not hungry.

4 **A:** It's cold in here.
 B: I *'ll close / close* the window.

5 Don't buy him that pink shirt – he *isn't liking / won't like* it.

6 I *'ll play / 'm playing* tennis after school today, so I *'ll be / 'm* home later than usual.

5 Look at the questions. Which form of the future shoul
you use to answer them?

1 What are you doing this weekend?

2 What time does school finish today?

3 What time will you go to sleep tonight?

4 Your friend says, 'This exercise is too hard!' What ca
you suggest?

6 Work in pairs. Ask and answer the questions.

Vocabulary

Adjectives

1 Francesca writes reviews for the school website. Complete her reviews with the words in the box.

> amazing ~~awesome~~ boring horrible
> interesting terrible

Winning Voices ★★★★★

Winning Voices was great fun last night. The Pictures won first prize. I'm glad because they were (1) .....*awesome*.....!

The Art of the Camera ★★★

Do you like digital photography? This show is quite (2) i............................, but I prefer paintings.

Student art exhibition ★★

I like paintings, but this exhibition isn't very good. It's just a bit (3) b............................

The King's Wife ★

The acting was bad. The costumes were bad. Everything was bad! Don't go. It's (4) t............................!

Star Wars: The Last Jedi ★★★★

This was the third time I've seen this (5) a............................ film. It never gets old!

Peter and the Rabbit

I didn't want to see this film, but my friend did, so I went with her. It was (6) h............................ No stars. Save your money!

2 Which adjectives from Exercise 1 mean *good*? Which
adjectives mean *bad*?

3 Work in pairs. Discuss these things.

• the last film you saw

• the last book you read

• the last TV programme you watched

> What was the last film you saw?

> What did you think of it?

> Moana.

> It was awesc

Writing Part 7

▶ **Page 141 Writing bank**
Writing Part 7

Write the past tense of each verb. Which pictures can you use these verbs with?

1	watch	....	**4**	go	....
2	see	....	**5**	decide	....
3	arrive	....	**6**	eat	....

Match the nouns with the pictures.

> bus stop   cinema   home   poster   TV

Use the past simple in your story.

Look at each picture and decide which verbs you need to say what happened.
Do you know the past tense of each verb?

Decide what nouns you need to tell the story.

Exam advice

Use the pictures to write the story.

Speaking Part 2

▶ **Page 147 Speaking bank**
Speaking Part 2

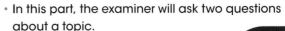

- In this part, the examiner will ask two questions about a topic.
- Remember to answer the questions as fully as possible, and give reasons.

Exam advice

1 Match words 1–5 with pictures A–E.

1	classical concert	**4**	ballet
2	film	**5**	play
3	rock concert		

2 Which kind of show from Exercise 1 do you like best?

3 Listen to the conversation and complete the questions the examiner asks Rita and Mario. Who gives the best answers?

56

1 Do you prefer going to shows with your .... or with your .... ?

2 What kind of .... would you like to go and see in the future?

4 Change Rita's short answers into fuller ones, using *because.*

1 My family. I love them.
I prefer going with ....

2 A rock concert. It will be exciting.
I'd like to see ....

5 Work in pairs. Ask and answer the questions from Exercise 3. Don't forget to give reasons with *because*.

10 It's going to be sunny

A

D

B

C

Starting off

1. Look at the photos. What can you see?

2. Match the seasons with photos A–D.

   spring   summer   autumn   winter

3. Listen to four students talking about their favourite seasons. Which season do they like the most?

   1 ....   3 ....
   2 ....   4 ....

57

4. Work in pairs.

   1 How many seasons does your country have?
   2 Which months are in which seasons in your country?
   3 Which is your favourite season? Why?

Listening Part 1

- Before you listen, look at all three pictures for each question and think about what you see.

- If you don't know the answer, you should choose one anyway – it might be correct!

Exam advice

1. Look at questions 1–5 and underline the key words.

You will hear five short conversations. For each question, choose the correct answer.

1 When is Holly visiting her friend in Japan?

  **B** 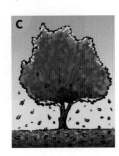 **C**

2 What is Frances doing on Sunday evening?

  **B**  **C**

3 What time does Lynn need to leave her class?

  **B**  **C**

4 How much is the book they buy?

  **B**  **C**

5 Who will meet Lee at the airport?

  **B**  **C**

Vocabulary

What's the weather like?

1 Match the weather phrases (1–5) with the pictures (A–E).

1 It's cold.   **4** It's snowing.
2 It's foggy.   **5** It's hot.
3 It's windy.

A  **B**  **C**

D 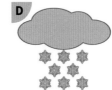 **E**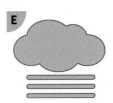

2 59 Listen. Write the temperatures for tomorrow on the map.

3 Work in pairs.

1 What is the weather like now, where you are?
2 What was the weather like yesterday?
3 What is the weather going to be like tomorrow?

Grammar

going to

▶ **Page 123 Grammar reference**
going to

1 Work in pairs. Read the conversation.

1 Why does Tony want to go to the park?
2 Why doesn't Juan want to go out?

Tony: Do you want to come to the park?

Juan: No, thanks.

Tony: Why not? Millie and Soraya are going to be there!

Juan: I'd like to, but it's a bit cold. And look at the sky– it's going to rain.

Tony: I've got an umbrella.

Juan: Sorry, Tony. I'm not going to leave the house today.

Tony: What are you going to do?

Juan: I'm going to stay in and watch some films.

Tony: OK. Maybe I'll see you tomorrow.

2 Match the rules (a–b) with the examples (1–2).

Rules

1 *Millie and Soraya are going to be there.*
2 *Look at the sky – it's going to rain.*
a We use *going to* + verb when we have information in the present that tells us what will happen in the future.
b We use *going to* + verb to talk about plans and intentions.

3 Match the uses of *going to* from Exercise 1 with rules a and b.

4 Complete the sentences with *(not) going to* and the verbs in brackets.

1 I think it's *going to snow* (snow) tomorrow.
2 Goodnight. I .... (go) to bed.
3 Susan........................ (wear) her new dress to the party tonight.
4 It .... (not rain) this weekend. Don't worry!
5 We .... (not walk) home after school. It's going to rain today.
6 You .... (like) this. It's brilliant!

5 Write questions and answers.

1 he / go / outside ?

Is he going to go outside?
No, he isn't. He's going to stay in.

2 he / swim / in the river ?

3 she / climb / a tree ?

4 they / have / a picnic?

5 it / be sunny / today?

6 **/P/** *going to*

 60 Listen and repeat the two ways of saying *going to*

Listen and practise saying the sentences.

1 I'm going to be there.
2 Look at the sky. It's going to rain.
3 I'm not going to leave the house today.
4 What are you going to do?
5 I'm going to stay in and watch some films.

Write four questions to ask your partner. Use *going to* and words from each group.

What	wear	after school today
Where	do	this evening
Who	play	tomorrow morning
When	meet	next summer
	go	this weekend
	call	

What are you going to do after school today?

Work in pairs. Ask and answer the questions.

HOLIDAY ACTIVITIES

- The questions are not in the same order as they appear in the texts.
- Read each question, and then look quickly at each text to decide which one has the answer you need.

Exam advice

1 Do you like going on holiday with your family? What sort of things do you enjoy doing?

2 For each question, choose the correct answer.

		Marta	Amy	Clara
1	Who had to go to a shop in the morning?	A	B	C
2	Who did an activity that happens at any time of year?	A	B	C
3	Who didn't have lunch during her activity?	A	B	C
4	Who ended an activity when she wanted?	A	B	C
5	Who gives advice about what to wear?	A	B	C
6	Who left early in the morning?	A	B	C
7	Who went with someone who explained things to her?	A	B	C

Marta

...riend and I rented bikes. It was easy. ...ked online and we collected the ...s and helmets from the shop after ...e breakfast. The bike shop is only ...n in the summer – I guess they ...t get many customers in the winter. ...e's a beautiful lake to cycle round ...great views of the mountains, but ...pretty tired and hungry. You can ...rn the bike any time you need, so I ...back at 2.30 and had lunch.

Amy

We took a boat trip to a nearby island. We had to get up before it got light to catch the boat – it went at 6.30 am. The captain told us that they only go out in good weather – and not at all in the winter months. Although it was July, we were still pretty cold – so don't forget a warm coat. We spent a few hours on the island, ate the sandwiches we brought with us, and came back at about 5 pm.

Clara

My friends and I love walking, so we went on a walking tour. It started at 10 am. They do them in all weathers, all year round. It was interesting because we needed to use maps and find our own way! The walk lasted three hours, through the forest and along the beach, and we had lunch too. Our guide was interesting – he knew everything about the island! At the end, there's a little shop where you can buy T-shirts and stuff.

Vocabulary
Places

1. Complete the quiz questions with the words below. Then answer the questions. Check on page 150.

> beach   desert   forest   islands   lake   mountain

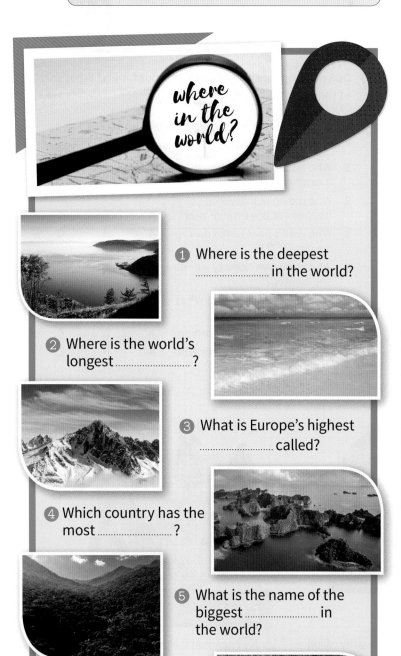

where in the world?

① Where is the deepest .... in the world?

② Where is the world's longest .... ?

③ What is Europe's highest .... called?

④ Which country has the most .... ?

⑤ What is the name of the biggest .... in the world?

⑥ Which is the world's hottest .... ?

2. Do you have any of the places from the box in Exercise 1 in your country? What are they called?

Grammar
must / mustn't

▶ **Page 124 Grammar reference**
must / mustn't

1. Look at this fact file about the highest mountain in Wales, Snowdon. Imagine you are going to walk up Snowdon. Make a list of things you need.

Location: Wales
Height: 1,085 metres

2. Read Laura's blog. Tick (✓) the things you must do. Cross (✗) the things you mustn't do.

I climbed Snowdon – why don't you?

So, last weekend I finally climbed Snowdon – the highest mountain in England and Wales! Here is my advice if you want to do the same.

First, decide what path to take to the top. There are a few of them – some harder than others. You mustn't pick one that's too hard for you, or you might get into trouble.

Plan your day carefully. Getting to the top and down again w take all day, so you must start early. Wear good strong boots and warm clothes. It can get really cold up there! Oh, and don't forget your phone – you might need to call for help.

You need energy to keep going all day, so you mustn't forget bring food and drink with you to have on the way up.

You must check the weather forecast before you start. If it's bad, don't go. If you're halfway up and the weather turns ba don't be afraid to turn back and come another day. The mountain will still be there tomorrow!

- plan your day
- choose a good path
- do it in any weather
- be afraid to turn back
- leave your phone at home
- wear strong boots
- start late in the day

3. Complete the rule and the examples below.

Rules

We use *must* and *mustn't* + ... to talk about obligation or strong advice in a formal way.

You .... start early.

You .... pick one that's too hard for you.

Look at the signs. What are they saying? Use *You must* or *You mustn't* and words from the box.

be careful   eat   ~~stop~~   use your phone

1      *You must stop*

2   ....

3   ....

4   ....

Work in pairs. What things must or mustn't you do in these places?

in a hospital   in a museum   in your school
on a bike   on a plane

eaking Part 1

▶ **Page 146 Speaking bank**
Speaking Part 1

Exam advice

• The examiner is speaking to you. Look at the examiner when you answer. You don't need to talk to your partner.

• If you don't understand, ask the examiner to repeat the question.

Look at these topics. What questions do you think an examiner will ask? Write two questions for each topic.

holidays   school   weekends

Listen to an examiner talking to two candidates. Write down the questions she asks.

1   What .... on holiday?
2   Who .... on holiday with?
3   What .... at the weekend?
4   What .... friends at the weekend?
5   What .... class in school?
6   Do you have .... at school?

62

Listen again. Tick the phrases you hear.

asking someone to repeat something	when you don't know what to say
Sorry, could you repeat that? Once again, please. Can you say that again, please?	Um … let me think. Well, I guess … That's a good question …

4 Work in pairs. Ask and answer the questions from Exercises 1 and 2.

Reading Part 5

Exam advice

• Always read the whole text before trying to fill the spaces.

• When the space is the first word of a question, it might be a form of *do*, *have* or *be*.

1 Complete each question with one word.

1   ....*Do*....... you like camping?
2   .... you going to watch TV tonight?
3   .... Sammy got a computer?
4   .... you go to the party last week?
5   .... you sleeping when I phoned you?
6   .... Marco want to come with us?

2 Look at the email. What kind of text is it? What does the writer want to say?

3 For each question, write the correct answer. Write one word for each gap.

Hi Sondra,

(0) ....*How*......... are you? I'm writing from the hotel room. We're near the beach, but the weather is terrible! It started raining on (1) .... day we arrived, and it looks (2) .... it isn't going to stop. (3) .... you hear about the storm we had last night? I thought the hotel was going to blow away!

Dad's happy. He likes walking, and he isn't worried (4) .... getting wet. But Mum isn't enjoying herself at all. (5) .... wants to go home, and I agree. This isn't fun!

(6) .... you still thinking about where to go on holiday? Take my advice. Don't come here!

Love, Carol

Grammar

1 Exam candidates often make mistakes with the *-ing* form and *to* infinitives. Correct the mistake in each sentence.

1 I'd like to go to the party because I enjoy ~~dance~~. *dancing*

2 Thank you for help me with this.

3 We decided to bought a new TV.

4 I would like visiting your country.

5 Stefan wants going to the seaside today.

6 I hope hearing from you soon.

7 We've got a little table for play cards.

8 After see the film, I will go to the café.

2 Complete the sentences with the *-ing* form or *to* infinitive of the verb in brackets.

1 I promise ...... *to phone* ...... (phone) you as soon as I get home.

2 Can you finish .... (wash) the car before Dad comes back?

3 Do you think Martin would like .... (come) with us to the beach?

4 I don't mind .... (walk) to school when it's sunny.

5 Are you going to learn .... (drive) when you are 16?

6 Susan looks really happy about .... (pass) all her exams.

3 Choose the correct options to complete the email.

Hi, Tim

I'm really looking forward to watching the tennis match with you on Saturday. **(1)** (*It'll be*) / *It is* great.

(2) *I'll meet* / *I'm meeting* you at the front door at 10.30 am. Don't worry, I **(3)** *won't be* / *am not* late this time! I know the match **(4)** *starts* / *is starting* at 11!

After the match, **(5)** *I'll meet* / *I'm meeting* my mum at about 2 pm, so I **(6)** *will need* / *am needing* to leave straight away. I **(7)** *won't have* / *am not having* time to have lunch with you, sorry. **(8)** *We go* / *We're going* to see my grandparents, who aren't very well at the moment.

Lisa

4 Put the words in the correct order to make questions. Then write short answers. Use the correct form of *will*.

1 snow / Will / tomorrow / it ? ✗
Will it snow tomorrow?
No, it won't.

2 be / the party / Susan / Will / at ? ✓
....
....

3 the shops / open / Will / on Sunday / be ? ✗
....
....

4 you / to football practice / Will / tomorrow / go ? ✓
....
....

5 Daniel / Will / next week / the race / win ? ✗
....
....

Vocabulary

5 Circle the correct option in *italics* to complete the dialogues.

1 **A:** *Why* / *Would* don't we go to the theatre?
B: I'd *think* / *rather* not.

2 **A:** *Shall* / *Would* you like to go to a cricket match?
B: Yeah, *sure* / *good*.

3 **A:** *How* / *Shall* about having chicken for dinner?
B: I don't *think* / *rather* so.

4 **A:** *Shall* / *Would* we watch a DVD?
B: Good *thanks* / *idea*!

6 Complete the sentences with adjectives from Unit 9.

1 I fell asleep in the film because it was so b*oring*

2 What an a .... goal!

3 This book is quite i............................ – why don't you r it?

4 What t............................ weather! Let's stay at home t

5 Don't order the soup. It's h.............................

Grammar

Put the words in the correct order to complete the conversation.

Jim: Hi, Kerry. What are you doing?

Kerry: I'm packing. (1) *We're going to go to Scotland tomorrow.* (to Scotland / going to / We're / tomorrow / go)

Jim: Oh, that's nice. (2) .... (going to / you / fly / Are ?)

Kerry: (3) .... (aren't / No, / fly / we / going to). I'm afraid of flying!
(4) .... (drive / is / going to / My dad).

Jim: (5) .... (you / stay / Where / going to / are)?

Kerry: In a tent!

Jim: (6) .... (fun / going to / That's / be)

Kerry: I hope so!

Complete the sentences with *must/mustn't* and verbs from the box.

> be   drink   ~~try~~   ride   send
> open   talk   go

1 She failed her test again. She ...*must try*... harder.
2 Hurry up! We .... late for school.
3 Shh! You .... in the exam.
4 The children .... to bed now, or they'll be tired in the morning.
5 I'm so thirsty. I .... something.
6 I'll give you your present now – but you .... it before your birthday!
7 It was nice to meet you. You .... me your email address.
8 You .... your bike here – it's too dangerous.

Vocabulary

Choose the correct option, A, B or C.

1 We don't need to wear our coats because it's going to be .... today.

   A hot   **B** cold   **C** foggy

2 It was so .... that my hat came off!

   A sunny   **B** windy   **C** hot

3 We couldn't go skiing because it didn't .... enough.

   A rain   **B** snow   **C** wind

4 It's .... Don't forget your umbrella!

   A foggy   **B** snowing   **C** raining

5 Please turn on the heating. It's really .... in here.

   A hot   **B** cold   **C** sunny

6 It is so .... outside, I can't see the other side of the street!

   A foggy   **B** windy   **C** hot

4 **Complete the crossword with words from Unit 10.**

Across

3 This is very high and there is often snow on the top of it.
6 You must travel over water to get to this.
9 Summer, for example.
10 There are a lot of trees in this place.

Down

1 People like to go to this place next to the sea.
2 summer, ..., winter
4 winter, ..., summer
5 This is water which moves from the land to the sea.
7 An area of water with land all around it.
8 A very hot place where it doesn't rain much.

11 I like to keep fit

Starting off

1 Work in pairs. Match the sentences (1–5) with the photos (A–E). Do you think the sentences are true or false?

1 A healthy teenager needs about 60 minutes of exercise every day.
2 Eight hours sleep per night is enough for most teenagers.
3 Being healthy can help you get good marks at school.
4 Washing your hands is important if you want to stay healthy.
5 Fast food is never healthy

2 Listen to the interview and check.

🎧 63

3 Work in pairs.

1 Are you a healthy person?
2 What unhealthy things do you do?
3 What do you do to keep fit?

Reading Part 3

1 Look at the photo.

1 Where are the people?
2 What are they doing?
3 What does a personal trainer do?

> • If you don't understand a word, try to guess its meaning from the words around it.
>
> • Read each of the three options carefully. Then decide which ones are wrong, and why.
>
> **Exam advice**

2 Read the article about a personal trainer. For each question, choose the correct answer.

Personal TRAINER

9-year-old Martha Larsen has been a personal trainer for over year. When she was younger, she wanted to be a footballer, ut she broke her leg at the age of 16, and a football career was ot possible anymore. 'I was sad at first,' she says. 'So my mum nd dad suggested I join a gym. I grew to love that, and soon I vas helping others get started.'

efore long, people were coming to Martha for help. Now she as over 40 students – some more than twice her age! She elieves she offers something other trainers do not. 'With me, 's not just about getting fitter,' she says. As well as making er students train very hard, she helps them think about what ney eat. 'Eating healthily is so important. If I do my job well, my tudents will sleep, work and play better.'

VHAT ADVICE WOULD MARTHA GIVE OMEONE WHO WANTS TO GET FIT?

he most important thing is not to wait until you can pay for personal trainer. The time to begin is now. Start slowly with ort runs, and go further each day. Soon you'll be ready for e gym.'

artha still lives with her parents, but she doesn't want to stay ere for too long. 'A lot of personal trainers dream of moving Hollywood and getting rich by training the stars,' she says. I be happy if I make enough money to buy my own flat. I don't ed to change.'

1 Martha became a personal trainer because
  A she could no longer be a football player.
  B she went to the gym when she was very young.
  C she knew other personal trainers.

2 What does Martha believe makes her different from other personal trainers?
  A She makes her students do more difficult exercises.
  B She has students who are much older than her.
  C She gives her students advice about food.

3 What advice does Martha give to someone who wants to get fit?
  A join a gym
  B find a trainer
  C start immediately

4 What does Martha hope to do in the future?
  A Get her own place to live.
  B Move to another country.
  C Train famous people.

5 What is the writer doing in this article?
  A giving advice about choosing a personal trainer
  B describing the life of a personal trainer
  C explaining how to become a personal trainer

3 Would you like a personal trainer to help you? Why? What would you like them to help you with?

Grammar
First conditional

▶ Page 125 Grammar reference
First conditional

1 Look at these sentences. Are they talking about the present or the future?

1 If I do my job well, my students will sleep, work and play better.
2 I'll be happy if I make enough money to buy my own flat.

2 Listen and complete the conversation between Martha Larsen and the journalist who interviewed her.

64

Journalist:	Thank you for the interview, Martha. That was very interesting.
Martha:	You're welcome.
Journalist:	So, could you be my personal trainer? I need to get fit.
Martha:	If you **(1)** .... me to be your personal trainer, I **(2)** .... be very happy to help you.
Journalist:	I should tell you I'm very lazy, and I don't like to work too hard.
Martha:	Ha ha! You **(3)** .... get fit if you **(4)** .... work hard!
Journalist:	Oh well, never mind!

3 The sentences in Exercises 1 and 2 are often called the first conditional. Complete the rules with *present* or *possible*.

> **Rules**
>
> 1 We use the first conditional to talk about what will happen in .... situations.
> 2 We form the first conditional with *if* + the .... tense, and *will* (or *won't*) + infinitive.

4 Match each sentence beginning (1–6) with its ending (a–e).

1 If you don't exercise,
2 You'll be tired tomorrow
3 What will Sam do
4 If I eat too much cake,
5 She won't let us eat
6 If you go running in the rain,

a if he doesn't go to school today?
b you'll get wet.
c if we don't wash our hands.
d I'll feel sick.
e you won't get fit.
f if you don't go to bed now.

5 Exam candidates often make mistakes with the first conditional. Correct the mistake in each sentence.

1 If I ~~won't~~ keep exercising, I won't get fit. *don't*
2 You like the class if you come.
3 If the weather is cool, will be very good.
4 I'll happy if you can come.
5 If someone want to call me, they will.
6 I think you feel better if you will eat better.

6 Complete the sentences so they are true for you.

1 If I drink lots of cola tonight,
   ....
2 I'll be very happy if
   ....
3 My parents will be pleased if
   ....
4 If I get up too early tomorrow,
   ....
5 If the weather is good this weekend,
   ....
6 If I don't do my homework tonight,
   ....

7 **/P/ Sentences with *if***

Listen and repeat Martha's sentences. Notice the paus[e] after the comma.

• If you want me to be your personal trainer, I'll be happ[y] to help you.

• You won't get fit if you don't work hard.

8 Complete these *If* clauses with your own words.

• If I met my favourite film star, ...
  ....
• If I missed the bus, ...
  ....
• If it rains, ...
• If the teacher leaves the class early, ...
  ....

9 Work in pairs. Practise saying the sentences.

> **Vocabulary**
> **Parts of the body**

1 Match the words from the box with body parts A–L i[n] the photos.

> arm   back   eye   finger   foot   hand   head
> leg   mouth   neck   nose   stomach

Which parts of the body are most important for these activities?

- running
- throwing and catching
- reading
- eating

Work in pairs. Student A think of a body part. Student B try to guess what it is by asking questions.

Do you use them for running?

No.

Do you use it for eating?

Yes!

A

B

C

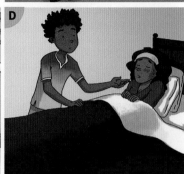

D

E

istening Part 4

Before listening, match questions 1–5 with pictures A–E.

For these questions, choose the correct answer. Then listen and check again.

1   You will hear a girl leaving a message about a football match. Why is she unhappy?

   A   She didn't play well.

   B   Her team lost.

   C   She was hurt.

2   You will hear a father talking to his daughter. Where have they been?

   A   in a hospital

   B   in a café

   C   on a bus

3   You will hear a mother talking to her son about school. Which subject is he getting better at?

   A   history

   B   Spanish

   C   maths

4   You will hear a mother talking to her son. What does the boy offer to do?

   A   make dinner

   B   go shopping

   C   clean the house

5   You will hear a boy leaving a message. Why does he want a lift home?

   A   His head hurts.

   B   His legs are tired.

   C   He has a temperature.

Grammar

something, anything, nothing, etc.

▶ **Page 126 Grammar reference**
something, anything, nothing, etc.

1   **Work in pairs.**

   1   What can help you concentrate in class?

   2   What things can make it difficult to concentrate?

   concentrate /kɒnsəntreɪt/ *verb*
   to think very hard about the thing you are doing and nothing else
   *Be quiet – I'm trying to **concentrate**.*

2 Read the article. What is unusual about the school?

A teacher in Australia has found a way for her students to keep fit and concentrate – and they don't have to do <u>anything</u>. They just have to sit at their desks! Instead of sitting on chairs, <u>everyone</u> in Miss Gray's class sits on large, soft exercise balls.

<u>Nothing</u> like this has been tried in classrooms before – but Miss Gray thinks it works. The students study better.

'<u>Someone</u> told me about these balls years ago. It is <u>something</u> I have wanted to try for a long time,' says Miss Gray. 'The students are happy, the parents are happy – <u>everyone</u> loves the new exercise balls! <u>No one</u> wants to sit on those boring old chairs now.'

Do you know <u>anyone</u> who uses one of these balls to sit on?

Write and let us know!

3 Complete the table with the <u>underlined</u> pronouns.

positive statements	negative statements
everyone	

4 Match the words (1–3) to the meanings (a–c).

1 everyone, everything
2 someone/anyone, something/anything
3 no one, nothing

a not all, or it doesn't matter which
b all
c none

5 Exam candidates often make mistakes with *any-*, *some-*, *no-* pronouns. Correct the mistake in each sentence.

1 I'll find anyone to help you. *someone*
2 We are going to get some to eat and drink.
3 We don't have to bring any thing with us.
4 I only paid 100 euros for everythings.
5 I love my room because I have all I like there.

Vocabulary
What's the matter?

1 Match the phrases (1–7) with the pictures (A–G).

1 I feel sick. A
2 I've got a temperature.
3 I've got a cold.
4 I've got toothache.
5 My leg hurts.
6 I've got a headache.
7 I've got a broken arm

2 Complete the sentences with words from the box.

drink   down   go (x2)   nothing   rest   take

1 .... an aspirin.
2 Lie .... in bed for a while.
3 .... to the dentist.
4 There's .... you can do, except rest.
5 .... some water.
6 .... to the doctor.
7 You need to ....

3 Work in pairs. Give each other advice about the problems from Exercise 1.

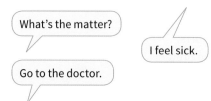

What's the matter?

I feel sick.

Go to the doctor.

peaking Part 2

▶ **Page 147 Speaking bank**
Speaking Part 2

> • Listen carefully to what your partner says and try to respond to their questions.
>
> • Talk to your partner, not the examiner!
>
> **Exam advice**

Do you like these healthy activities? Say why or why not.

Listen to two students talking about the pictures. Complete the questions they ask each other.

1   Do you ....*eat*.......... a lot of vegetables?
2   What .... you?
3   How .... do you sleep for?
4   .... you ever go running?
5   .... not?
6   What do you .... about that?
7   .... you .... cycling?
8   What .... ?
9   .... ?

Work in pairs. Ask and answer the questions from Exercise 2. Don't forget to ask follow-up questions.

> What about you?

> Why/Why not?

> What do you think about...?

Writing Part 6

▶ **Page 139 Writing bank**
Writing Part 6

> • Always check your work when you have finished.
>
> **Exam advice**

1 Underline the questions in this email from a friend.

> Hi Mario,
>
> Yes, I would love to come for a run in the park with you. What time shall we meet at your house? How are we going to get to the park? What will we do if it rains?
>
> Gina

2 Read the replies and answer the questions.

1   Who wrote under 25 words?
2   Who didn't include all three pieces of information?
3   Who made the most spelling mistakes?
4   Who needs to check their grammar?
5   Who didn't start their message correctly?
6   Who will get the best mark?

> Hi Gina,
>
> Thanks for the message. Let's meet in 2 o'clock at my house tomorrow. If it will rain, we will go to the café near the park.
>
> Mario

> Hello Gina,
>
> I'm glad you can come. We'll meet at 1.30 at my house. We can walk to the park because it's not far. We'll stay inside and play games if it rains.
>
> Best wishes
>
> Tony

> Let's meet at my haus 1 o'clock. We can run to the park. If it rains, we will to take the buse
>
> Stefan

3 Work in pairs. Correct the mistakes in Mario's and Stefan's emails.

4 Write your own email to Gina.

12 Have you ever been on a plane?

A | C | D | B | E | F

Starting off

Means of transport

1 Listen and match the sounds (1–6) with
the forms of transport in the photos (A–F).

🎧 68

| **A** boat | **B** plane | **C** bike |
| **D** bus | **E** car | **F** train |

2 Listen and tick (✓) how the students get to school.
How long does it take?

🎧 69

	by car	by boat	by bike	by bus	How long?
John					.... minutes
Karen					.... minutes
Jordan					.... minutes

3 Work in pairs. Ask and answer the questions.

1 How do you get to school?
2 How long does it take?

eading Part 1

Exam advice

- If you don't understand a word, try to guess its meaning from the words around it.
- Read each option carefully. Decide which ones are wrong and why.

For each question, choose the correct answer.

1

BOAT TRIPS!
Half-price for groups of 10 or more.
Ask at the shop.

A You will pay more to do this alone.
B You have to be over 10 to do this.
C You will enjoy this more with friends.

2

Beautiful old skateboard for sale.
Four years old – needs new wheels!
£10 or nearest offer.
Phone Daniel   09892 393909

A The skateboard is for a young child.
B The skateboard is ready to ride.
C The price of the skateboard can be changed.

3

Hi Amy,

I'm ill, so I'm staying at home. Could you tell Mrs Jenkins, the new English teacher? Message me if we have homework.

Ollie

What does Ollie want Amy to do?
A Go to Ollie's house.
B Talk to Mrs Jenkins.
C Help Ollie with his homework.

4

Takeaway Café
Healthy drinks and snacks.
Closed weekends.
Friendly staff.

A The café sells food that is very cheap.
B The café is open on Sundays.
C The café has nice people working there.

5

Maddie,

A new dance class is starting at school. It's for people our level, not beginners. I'll tell you more after music class.

Anna

A There is a new dance school in town.
B Anna and Maddie have done dance before.
C The new dance class begins after the music lesson.

6

Lost bike helmet (green)
I left it at school. It was cheap, but I love it!
Email greg121@mailbank.com

Greg wants his bike helmet back because
A He likes it a lot.
B It was expensive.
C It is his favourite colour.

Grammar
Present perfect

▶ **Page 127 Grammar reference**
Present perfect

1 Do you like long car journeys? Why? / Why not?

2 Look at the photos. What do you think the article is about?

DO YOU LIKE LONG CAR JOURNEYS?

The Zapp family from Argentina do. They started their journey in 2000, and they are still travelling!

Mr and Mrs Zapp <u>have travelled</u> more than 320,000 kilometres in their old car. Their four children were all born in different countries: Pampa is a U.S. citizen, Tehue is Argentinian, Paloma is Canadian, and Wallaby is Australian. The children <u>have been</u> to schools in different countries, and they <u>have learned</u> a lot of things on their journey round the world.

The family <u>has been</u> to more than 75 different countries, and thousands of people <u>have invited</u> them into their homes. Maybe they <u>have visited</u> a place near you. <u>Have you seen</u> them?

Have you ever been on a plane?

3 Read the sentences and answer the questions.

> Mr and Mrs Zapp have travelled more than 320,000 kilometres in their old car.

1 Does this sentence talk about something that started in the past and continues to now?

> The children have been to schools in different countries, and they have learned a lot of things…

2 Do we know exactly when the Zapp children learned those things?

4 Look at the <u>underlined</u> examples of the present perfect in the article. Then complete the rules .

> have   past   when

Rules

1 We use the present perfect to talk about experiences in the .... with a link to the present.

2 When we use the present perfect to talk about experiences, we do not say exactly .... they happened.

3 We form the present perfect with .... / *has* + past participle.

5 Complete the sentences with the present perfect form of the verb in brackets.

1 I ..*have visited*.. (visit) lots of countries.

2 Most people .... (never / jump) out of a plane.

3 My brother .... (cook) lots of meals this year.

4 You .... (not / play) basketball before, have you?

5 My uncle .... (stay) in some very expensive hotels on business.

6 We .... (study) for six hours today, and we still .... (not / finish).

6 Some past participles are irregular. Complete the sentences with past participles from the box.

> driven   drunk   eaten (x2)
> ~~read~~   stopped   swum   written

1 I have ....*read*........ all of the Harry Potter books.

2 Have you ever .... a car?

3 My teacher has .... a letter to my parents.

4 It hasn't .... raining for days.

5 I feel bad because I've .... too much.

6 Who has .... all the orange juice?

7 Have you ever .... any unusual food?

8 Sonja's never .... in the sea.

7 Listen to the Zapp family talking about their experiences on the road. Choose the correct answer.

1 Have the Zapps ever had problems on their journey

  A Yes, they have.

  B No, they haven't.

2 Has the car ever stopped working?

  A Yes, it has.

  B No, it hasn't.

3 Has the car ever travelled faster than 55 kilometres per hour?

  A Yes, it has.

  B No, it hasn't.

4 Have the children seen any wild animals?

  A Yes, they have.

  B No, they haven't.

5 Have they ever been to Vietnam?

  A Yes, they have.

  B No, they haven't.

8 Make questions using *ever* and the present perfect. Write true answers. Then add two more questions of your own.

1 you / live in another country?

> *Have you ever lived in another country?*
> *Yes, I have. / No, I haven't.*

2 you / be / on a plane?

....

....

3 you / miss / a train or bus?

....

....

4 you / go / on a trip without your parents?

....

....

9 Work in pairs. Ask and answer the questions.

ocabulary
ehicles

Label the pictures with words from the box.

| coach | helicopter | motorbike | scooter | taxi | tram |

1 ....

2 ....

3 ....

4 ....

5 ....

6 ....

ules

You can travel, go or be <u>in</u> a taxi, car and helicopter.

You can travel, go or be <u>on</u> a coach, plane and scooter.

Complete the sentences so they are true for you.
Use words from Exercise 1.

1 I don't like travelling by ...
2 I prefer going by ...
3 I have often been on/in a ...
4 I have never been on/in a ...

---

3 Work in pairs. What are your favourite and least favourite forms of transport?

> What's your favourite form of transport?

> Why?

> I love travelling by plane.

> I love flying. Some people are frightened, but I love it! And you?

Listening Part 2

- Names are always spelled out. Make sure you know the alphabet in English!
- The answers follow the order of the recording.
- Do not waste time writing numbers as words.

Exam advice

1 Listen and write the times you hear.

🎧 71

1 ......10.45...... am
2 .... pm
3 .... pm
4 .... pm
5 .... pm

2 Imagine you are going to do a 10-kilometre run. What questions do you want to ask about it? Make questions using these words.

| clothes | distance | meet | time | weather | when |

3 Look at the notes. What kind of information do you need in each gap?

FUN RUN

Day: .....Saturday....
How far: **(1)** .... km
Weather: **(2)** ....
Should wear: **(3)** .... ,
T-shirt and trainers
Run begins: **(4)** .... am
Meeting place: **(5)** ....Park

4 For each question, write the correct answer in the gap. You will hear a teacher talking to her class about a countryside run they are doing. Write one word or a number or a date or a time.

🎧 72

5 Listen again and check.

🎧 72

Grammar
should / shouldn't

▶ **Page 128 Grammar reference**
should / shouldn't

1 Look at the sentences. Which word expresses advice or something you have to do?

1 You should wear something light and comfortable.
2 You should get there early.
3 You shouldn't worry.

2 Complete the bicycle safety notice. Use *should* or *shouldn't* and words from the box.

> carry passengers   cycle on the pavement
> listen to music   look behind you
> ride too close to parked cars   turn on your lights
> use the bike path   wear bright clothes

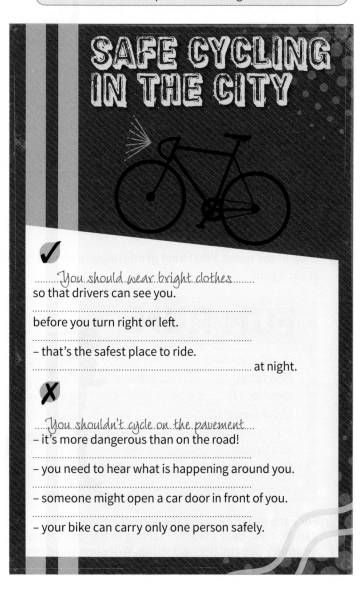

SAFE CYCLING IN THE CITY

✔

.........You should wear bright clothes.........
so that drivers can see you.

....
before you turn right or left.

....
– that's the safest place to ride.

....at night.

✘

.....You shouldn't cycle on the pavement....
– it's more dangerous than on the road!

....
– you need to hear what is happening around you.

....
– someone might open a car door in front of you.

....
– your bike can carry only one person safely.

3 **/P/** /ʃ/ and /tʃ/
Listen. Which sound is longer?

1 /ʃ/
2 /tʃ/

4 Listen and repeat the sentences.

1 You should check your work.
2 You shouldn't chat during lessons.
3 You should watch this show.
4 You should learn how to catch fish.

5 Listen again. Underline the /ʃ/ sounds and circle the /tʃ/ sounds in the sentences.

6 Work in pairs. Give each other advice in these situations. Use *should/shouldn't* and your own ideas.

- You feel very tired all the time.
- You are always late for school.
- You get bad marks in English.
- You don't understand the lesson.

> I feel very tired all the time.

> You should go to bed earlier

Vocabulary
Travel verbs

1 Match the vehicles from the box with verbs 1–3. Some vehicles go with more than one verb.

> a bicycle   a bus   a car   a coach   a helicopter
> a motorbike   a plane   a taxi   a train   a tram

1 drive *a car*
2 fly
3 ride

2 Choose the correct words in *italics*.

1 I'm learning to *drive / ride* a scooter.
2 My mum is a pilot. She *flies / drives* planes all over world.
3 Dan's uncle *rides / drives* a taxi in London.
4 I got on my bike and *rode / drove* home.
5 We got off the bus to the airport and then *drove / f* to Los Angeles in a big plane.

3 Work in pairs. Think of an interesting place you have visited. Imagine that your partner is visiting this pla Take turns to say how your partner should travel th

Writing Part 7

▶ **Page 141 Writing bank**
Writing Part 7

> • Give your characters names.
> • Write something about each picture.
> • It is better to use past tenses to tell your story in the exam.

Exam advice

Look at the three pictures below. What words do you need to say what happened? Make a list of the objects (nouns) and actions (verbs).

Match the words with the three pictures.

> breakfast kitchen eat birthday parents
> wait bus stop watch worry arrive bus
> friends music party

Now write your story. Write up to 65 words.

Speaking Part 1

▶ **Page 146 Speaking bank**
Speaking Part 1

> • If your partner does not understand your question, try to ask it in a different way.

Exam advice

1 Write each question in a different way. Use the word in brackets.

1 Where did you go last summer? (anywhere)
Did *you go anywhere last summer?*

2 How did you get there? (plane)
Did ....?

3 How do you go to school every day? (bus)
Do ....?

4 How long is the journey to school? (far)
Is ....?

2 Listen to an examiner talking to a candidate. Complete the information.

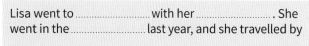

> Lisa went to .... with her .... She went in the .... last year, and she travelled by ....

3 Write three questions to ask your partner on the topic of travel and transport.

4 Work in pairs. Ask and answer your questions. If you don't understand a question, ask your partner to say it in a different way.

11 Vocabulary and grammar review

Grammar

1 Choose the correct option in *italics*.

1 If you (study) / will study hard, you will pass your exams.
2 If you don't go to school today, your teacher *will be / is* angry.
3 She'll be very happy if her parents *will buy / buy* her a bike.
4 If we *'ll go / go* to the cinema tomorrow, we'll take Rob with us.
5 We *'ll get / get* another drink if we're still thirsty later.
6 If we do our homework tonight, we *won't have / don't have* to do it at the weekend.

2 Write first conditional questions.

1 what / you / drink / if / you / be / thirsty / this evening?
What will you drink if you are thirsty this evening?
2 what / you / do / if / it / be / sunny tomorrow?
....
3 what / your parents / do / if / you / pass all your exams?
....
4 how / you / feel / if / you / eat / too much chocolate?
....
5 where / you / go / if / it / rain / this weekend?
....
6 who / you /ask / if / you / need help / with your homework?
....

3 Complete the words with *some*, *any*, *every* or *no*.

1 Hello? Is there *any*body here?
2 I've bought Dave ....thing great for his birthday. He'll love it.
3 We looked ....where, but we couldn't find our car.
4 ....body loves good food.
5 **A:** Where did you go last night?
B: ....where. I stayed in and watched TV.
6 ....body failed the test. The whole class passed!
7 I don't want ....thing to eat, thank you.
8 We want to go on holiday ....where hot and sunny this year.

Vocabulary

4 Complete the crossword with body words.

Across

3 You wear a shoe on this part of the body.
4 You smell things with this.
6 You use this to pick things up and write.
7 It's behind you!
8 Your hand is on the end of this.
9 The top part of your body.

Down

1 You put food in here when you eat.
2 This is where the food goes when it's inside you.
3 You have ten of these on your hands.
4 This is between your body and your head.
5 You use these to see.

5 Complete the sentences with words from Unit 11.

1 My head hurts. I've got a) *headache* .
2 My tooth hurts. I've got t......................... .
3 I'm hot. I've got a t......................... .
4 Ouch! I've h......................... my foot!
5 You can't go to school today. You've got a c......................... .
6 I feel s......................... .

Grammar

Write the past participles of these verbs.

1 drive   *driven*
2 buy   ....
3 read   ....
4 eat   ....
5 go   ....

Mike is going on a camping trip. Look at the list of things he has and hasn't done, and write sentences.

> buy the train ticket ✓
> make some sandwiches ✗
> clean the tent ✓
> buy a map ✗
> wash my clothes ✓
> invite Maria ✓
> find a cooking pot ✗

1 *He's bought the train ticket.*
2 ....
3 ....
4 ....
5 ....
6 ....
7 ....

Write questions and sentences with the present perfect.

1 You / drive / car?
   Have you ever driven a car?
2 I / never / eat / sushi.
   ....
3 My best friend / read / lots of books.
   ....
4 My brother / eat / too much chocolate.
   ....
5 they / ever / go / to Spain?
   ....
6 My dad / buy / a new car.
   ....

4 **Read the sentences, then write advice using *should* or *shouldn't*.**

1 I hurt my foot when I was jumping off my desk.
   You shouldn't jump off your desk!
2 Dani is great at football, but he doesn't practise very often.
   ....
3 I want to finish this book, but I'm tired and my eyes hurt.
   ....
4 These shoes are too small and they hurt my feet.
   ....
5 Using a tablet gives me a headache.
   ....
6 Steve doesn't like vegetable soup.
   ....

Vocabulary

5 **Put the letters in the correct order to make vehicles.**

1 AXIT   *Taxi*
2 USB   ....
3 ATBO   ....
4 NAPEL   ....
5 MART   ....
6 RECOSTO   ....
7 OTHILCREPE   ....
8 OMTEROIBK   ....

6 **Choose the correct option, A, B, or C.**

1 Have you ever ....*ridden*.... a scooter?
   A gone   **B** flown   **C** ridden
2 We .... to France in our old car.
   A drove   **B** flew   **C** rode
3 .... a plane is really difficult.
   A Driving   **B** Flying   **C** Riding
4 I'm learning to .... a bike – I have never learned before!
   A fly   **B** drive   **C** ride
5 Uncle Martin .... a helicopter when he was a policeman.
   A flew   **B** drove   **C** rode
6 The only vehicle Dad hasn't .... is a fire engine.
   A flown   **B** driven   **C** ridden

13 What's your hobby?

Starting off

1 Work in pairs. If you have some free time this weekend, what will you do?

2 Match the words with the pictures.

1 doing puzzles
2 playing computer games
3 making jewellery
4 snowboarding
5 sailing

3 Listen to a teacher asking Natasha about her hobbie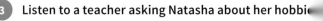

🎧 76
1 What were her hobbies when she was younger?
2 What are her hobbies now?
3 What hobby would she like to try?

4 What are your hobbies? Which hobby would you like try? Why?

Listening Part 3

Exam advice

- Don't choose an answer just because it has a word you hear in the recording.
- The answer will sometimes paraphrase something that you hear.

Work in pairs. Try to think of other ways of saying these things.

1 I'll text you. *I'll send you a message.*
2 There were too many people on the bus.
3 I did the puzzle in just over 10 minutes.
4 I went to the cinema.
5 I'll give you riding lessons.
6 My helmet wasn't big enough.
7 I'm getting much better at snowboarding.

You will hear paraphrases of the sentences in Exercise 2. Match the sentences you hear (a–g) with the sentences from Exercise 1.

> **paraphrase** *verb* [I,T]
> to say something that has been said or written in a different way
> 'I'll send you a message' is a paraphrase of 'I'll text you'.

Look at questions 1–5. <u>Underline</u> the key words.

1 When did Rich start riding?
   A two weeks ago
   B earlier today
   C last month

2 Rich thought his first lesson was
   A a bit boring.
   B too short.
   C difficult.

3 What did Jess have to borrow at her first riding lesson?
   A some boots
   B a hat
   C a jacket

4 Jess says her teacher was
   A an excellent rider.
   B a good teacher.
   C kind to children.

5 What does Rich plan to do in the future?
   A start another hobby
   B keep going to riding lessons
   C teach his friend to ride

4 **For each question, choose the correct answer. You will hear Rich talking to his friend Jess about horse riding.**

78

Grammar

Present perfect with *for* and *since*

▶ **Page 129 Grammar reference**
Present perfect with *for* and *since*

1 **Look at the photos. What are the people doing? Have you ever done anything like this?**

2 **Read the blog. What is Ben's hobby?**

I live in the city and during the week I go to a place called Adventure Zone. There are lots of things you can do there. They have indoor rock climbing, surfing and kayaking. I go indoor climbing every week.

I began climbing last year with my sister. We were on holiday in France and we made some new friends. They were mountain climbers, and we joined them. We had an awesome time! When we got home, my sister and I wanted to do more climbing. That's when we found Adventure Zone, which has an indoor climbing wall.

The wall has easy climbs and hard climbs. You practise on the easy parts first. Then, as you get stronger, you can try the more difficult ones. I've improved a lot since I began and now I can climb most of the wall easily.

I've lived in this town for five years and at first, I thought it was really boring. But I didn't know about Adventure Zone! Now I think I live in the best place! It's awesome.

3 Match the beginning of each sentence with its ending to complete the rules.

Rules

I've lived in this town for five years.
I've improved a lot since I began.

1 We use *for* with the present perfect to

2 We use *since* with the present perfect to

a talk about a period of time.

b say when something started.

4 Complete the sentences with *for* or *since*.

1 I have known my best friend ....*for*......... three years.
2 We've had the same sailing boat .... 2005.
3 My dance partner has been away .... weeks.
4 The riding school has been closed .... June.
5 My friends and I haven't been on a snowboarding holiday .... a long time.

5 Complete the sentences so that they are true for you.

1 I have known my best friend for
....

2 My family have lived here since
....

3 I have had these shoes for
....

4 I haven't had anything to eat since
....

5 I have been at this school for
....

6 Work in pairs. Write questions about the sentences from Exercise 5. Then ask and answer your questions.

How long have you known your best friend?

I've known my best friend for nine years.

Vocabulary
Adverbs

1 Read the sentences. Which <u>underlined</u> word describes the noun? Which describes the verb?

You practise on the <u>easy</u> parts first.
I can climb most of the wall <u>easily</u>.

2 Choose the correct words in *italics* to complete the interview with Ben.

Interviewer: Have you ever had a **(1)** *bad / badly* experience?

Ben: No, I haven't, but my friend Jim has. He w climbing a mountain when he fell **(2)** *bad / badly*. He broke his arm.

Interviewer: How long did it take to get better?

Ben: It got better quite **(3)** *quick / quickly*. He w lucky!

Interviewer: Is it **(4)** *easy / easily* to hurt yourself wher you are climbing?

Ben: If you're not **(5)** *careful / carefully,* you ca get hurt quite **(6)** *easy / easily*. You have t plan each climb **(7)** *careful / carefully*.

Interviewer: What advice would you give to someone who wants to learn to climb?

Ben: Find a **(8)** *good / well* teacher. I've never had a bad experience because my teach taught me **(9)** *good / well*.

3 Complete the table.

adjective	adverb
regular	
bad	
	carefully
	slowly
quick	
easy	
	happily
irregular	
	well

4 Complete each sentence with the adverb form of adjectives from the box.

bad   slow   easy   sad   good   ~~happy~~

1 The baby laughed ....*happily*....... at her new toy.
2 Please drive .... There are children play in the street.
3 Carla speaks English very .... because s was born in London.
4 Jake hurt himself .... while he was snow boarding.
5 We thought it would be difficult, but everyone completed the exercise ....
6 'I can't come to your party because I'm ill,' Sam sa ....

5 Work in pairs. Say which things from the box you do and which you do badly.

climb   cook   cycle   dance   paint   run   sing   s

eading Part 3

Do you play games? What games do you enjoy playing?

What game can you see in the photo? Read and check.

Go is a board game for two players. It began in China more than 2,500 years ago. You can play on a board with stones, or you can play online.

Read the article. For each question, choose the correct answer.

1 James has lived in South Korea for
   A five years.
   B eight years.
   C thirteen years.
2 Where did James learn how to play?
   A at home
   B in a club
   C at school
3 What does James like most about playing Go?
   A winning prizes
   B making new friends
   C visiting other countries
4 What does James enjoy watching on TV?
   A comedies
   B music videos
   C adventure films
5 What does James say about his future?
   A He wants to be the best player in the world.
   B He plans to do something different.
   C He wants to keep playing Go.

Teenage Go Player

James Kwak is a Go player. He has lived in South Korea since he was eight years old. His parents moved there with the whole family five years ago. Now, at the age of 13, many people think James could become one of the best Go players in the world.

James' mother is a good Go player, but James didn't learn until he was seven. 'Some of my friends wanted to join the local Go club even though none of them knew how to play!' he says. 'Luckily the PE teacher is a fantastic player – she taught us at lunch time.'

James loves to win competitions. In fact, he's made quite a lot of money, but that's not the most important thing to him. He travels around the world, too, but he says that can be tiring. 'The best thing is meeting lots of lovely people. We have loads of fun together.'

In his free time, James loves watching TV because he doesn't have to think! 'My friends like pop and rock videos, or superhero movies. I prefer the funny stuff. If it doesn't make me laugh, I'm not interested.'

He's not sure about what he'll do in the future. 'I don't think I will be the world's number-one player,' he says. 'But who knows?' He's thinking about going to university and studying to be a doctor. The one thing he knows for sure is that he'll never stop enjoying the game.

Best of luck, James!

4 **Have you ever played Go? Would you like to?**

Grammar
may / might

▶ **Page 129 Grammar reference**
may / might

1 Complete the rule with *sure* or *not sure*.

> ### Rules
>
> One day I **might** be the world's number one player.
>
> I **may** decide to go to university and become a doctor.
>
> I have a lot of homework, so I **might not** come out tonight.
>
> We use *may* (*not*) or *might* (*not*) when we are .... that something is true.

2 Complete the sentences with your own ideas. Use *may* (*not*) or *might* (*not*).

1 Tony's hobby is cooking.
  He ....*might be a chef when he grows up*............
2 There is somebody at the door.
  It ....
3 Dan isn't in school today.
  He ....
4 My friend hasn't replied to my message.
  He / She ....
5 I bought a lottery ticket yesterday.
  I ....

Vocabulary
Jobs

1 Look at the photos.
• What are the people doing?
• What jobs might they do in the future?

2 Match the students with the jobs they might enjoy doing in the future.

> coach   journalist   mechanic   nurse
> photographer   ~~pilot~~   vet

1 Suzy has always loved planes.   pilot
2 Daniel likes animals and wants to help them.
3 Julianna is always taking pictures with her phone.
4 Mariann loves football, and enjoys teaching.
5 Stefan is interested in the news and likes writing.
6 Juan wants to help people who are ill.
7 Pat loves fixing things, especially his bike.

3 **/p/** /w/ /v/ /b/
🎧 79 Listen. What is the first sound in each word?

> business   vet   waiter
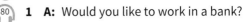

4 Complete the rules with /w/, /v/ or /b/.

> ### Rules
>
> For the .... sound, the mouth is closed at first.
>
> For the .... sound, the mouth is slightly open.
>
> For the .... sound, the bottom lip touches the top teet

5 Listen and repeat the conversations.
🎧 80
1 **A:** Would you like to work in a bank?
   B: No. That would be very boring. I want to be a ve
2 **A:** Vicky was a window cleaner. Now she's a very r
      businesswoman.
   B: Wow!
3 **A:** Victor makes videos for bands. They're wonder
   B: Yes, he does them very well.

6 Work in pairs. Which job would you like to do most? Which would you not like to do?

> I'd like to be a nurse, because I like looking after people. I wouldn't like …

Writing Part 6

▶ **Page 139 Writing bank**
Writing Part 6

> • Always check your work when you have finished.
>
> • Make sure you respond to all three points.

Exam advice

Read the exam task and the answer. Find four mistakes in the answer.

- one grammar mistake
- one spelling mistake
- one punctuation mistake
- one point which the writer didn't answer

You want to go shopping with your English friend, Maddy, on Saturday. Write an email to Maddy.

In your email:
- **ask** Maddy **to come with you**
- **tell** Maddy **where** to meet you
- say **what** she **should bring**

Hi Maddy,

Would you like to come shopping with me on Saturday. Let's meet at 10 o'clock outside the libary. I hope we will have a very nice time.

See you,

Federico.

Do the task below.

You want to go sailing on Saturday with your English friend, Bobbie. Write an email to Bobbie.

In your email:
- **ask** Bobbie to **go sailing with you on Saturday**.
- **say where** you want to go sailing.
- tell Bobbie **what** he **should take**.

Speaking Part 2

▶ **Page 147 Speaking bank**
Speaking Part 2

> • Remember there is no right or wrong answer – just say what you think.
>
> • You can ask the examiner to repeat something.

Exam advice

1 **Match the questions (1–3) with the answers (a–c).**

1 What are you going to do this weekend?
2 What job do you want to do in the future?
3 Are you going to study English at university?

a I haven't decided. I might not go to university.
b I don't know. Maybe I'll be a police officer.
c I'm not sure. I may go swimming.

2 **Work in pairs.**

1 Do you do any of the hobbies in the pictures?
2 Which hobbies do you think you would you like to do?

3 **Listen to an examiner asking two candidates some final questions. Complete the questions.**

81

1 When you're older, would you prefer to do an .... or an .... ?
2 What .... do you think you might like to do?

4 **Who gives the best answers, Sonya or Stefan?**

5 **Work in pairs. Discuss the questions from Exercise 3.**

What's your hobby?

14 Keep in touch!

IMPORTANT NOTICE.

Class 5C English is in Room 4 today. (2.25 start, as usual)

Starting off

1 **Work in pairs. Look at the pictures.**

- Do you use any of these ways of communicating? Which ones do you use most?
- Do you communicate differently with different people? How?
- Can you think of other ways of communicating?

Listening Part 5

1 **Think about a website that you like or use often.**

- Why do you visit it?
- Why do you like it?
- What information does it include?

2 **Work in pairs. What are the top three features of a g website? Think about these ideas, or your own.**

- lots of good pictures and videos
- easy to use
- useful and interesting information
- attractive design
- modern style

- When the words in the second column are adjectives, the speakers might paraphrase them.
- The names/words in the first list are in the order you hear them.
- The words in the second list are not in the order you hear them.

Exa
advi

3 **Match the adjectives (1–5) with their paraphrases (a**

1	modern	a	She tells jokes.
2	clear	b	This website is bad.
3	funny	c	It's very 21st-century!
4	slow	d	It's easy to understand.
5	terrible	e	It took a long time.

For these questions, choose the correct answer. You will hear Billy talking to Sian about a new school website. What was each person's opinion about the website?

People		Opinion about the website	
0	Rose A	**A**	boring
1	Jeremy	**B**	broken
2	Alex	**C**	clear
3	David	**D**	dark
4	Sandra	**E**	modern
5	Ruth	**F**	slow
		G	strange
		H	useful

Listen again and check.

Grammar

The passive

▶ **Page 130 Grammar reference**
The passive

Look at the language facts. How many did you know?

do we communicate?

...r 7,000 different languages <u>are spoken</u> in the world.

...ew word <u>is added</u> to the English dictionary every two days.

...English, the letter E <u>is used</u> more often than any other.

... of school time in Luxembourg <u>is spent</u> learning languages ...glish, French and German).

...glish <u>is studied</u> by more people than any other language.

...he 19th century, a new, international language called ...eranto <u>was invented</u>.

...first text message <u>was sent</u> in 1992. It said 'Merry ...istmas'.

...first emoji <u>was created</u> in Japan by Shigetaka Kurita.

...again at the facts in Exercise 1.

...we know who sent the first text message?

...we know who adds new words to the English dictionary?

...we know exactly who uses the letter E?

...we know who created the first emoji?

...ok at the <u>underlined</u> words. Which facts are in the present ...nse and which ones are in the past tense?

...se the correct options in *italics*.

Rules

1 We use the passive when we *know / don't know* who did the action, or it isn't important.

2 We use the passive with *by / on* when we want to say who does the action.

3 The passive is formed with the correct form of the verb *to be / to have* + past participle.

4 Tick (✓) the sentences that use the passive.

1 My phone was made in China. ✓
2 Sally sends hundreds of texts every day.
3 We are given too much homework at this school.
4 I wrote this email.
5 Who was this book written by?
6 People send billions of text messages every year.

5 Complete the report with the correct form of the passive.

When people communicate with each other on social media, they don't just use words – they use a variety of tiny pictures. These pictures (1) .... (call) emojis.

The first electronic emoji (2) .... (make) in Japan by a man called Shigetaka Kurita in 1999. He got his ideas from lots of things: street signs, manga comics, and the weather forecast symbols that (3) .... (show) on maps.

But the oldest emoji (4) .... (discover) in Turkey in 2017, when scientists found a 3,700 year old vase with a smiley face painted on it!

Although emojis (5) .... (use) a lot nowadays, sometimes they (6) .... (not / understand) by the people who receive them. I once sent this emoji 😊 to a friend. I (7) .... (surprise) when she wrote back: 'Why are you crying?'

6 Work in pairs. Try to choose the correct answers in *italics*. Then check your answers on page 150.

1 Spanish is spoken in *12 / 20 / 30* countries.
2 Writing was invented *320 / 3,200 / 32,000* years ago.
3 The first email was sent in *1971 / 1981 / 1991.*
4 820 different languages are spoken in *the USA / Malaysia / Papua New Guinea.*
5 The word most often spelled wrongly by Key students is *because / beautiful / tomorrow.*
6 Smartphones are used most often for *texting / phoning / checking the time.*

Vocabulary
Communication verbs

1 Match the underlined verbs with the definitions (a–h).

1 Will you two please stop <u>arguing</u> with each other. I'm trying to study.
2 I <u>chatted</u> with my friends all night.
3 Can you <u>describe</u> what the new student looks like?
4 After we watch a film together, we like to <u>discuss</u> it.
5 If you don't understand it, I'll be happy to <u>explain</u>.
6 I didn't want to go, but Anita <u>persuaded</u> me.
7 Can you <u>repeat</u> that please?
8 There's no need to <u>shout</u> – I can hear you clearly.

a to make someone agree to something by talking to them about it
b to speak angrily and disagree with someone
c to say or write what someone or something is like
d to say or do something more than once
e to talk with someone in a friendly and informal way
f to make something clear or easy to understand
g to say something very loudly
h to talk about something to someone and share your ideas and opinions

2 Listen and match the underlined verbs from Exercise 1 with the recordings (a–h).

83

a ......*repeat*......   e ....
b ....   f ....
c ....   g ....
d ....   h ....

3 Complete the sentences with verbs from Exercise 1.

1 Let's ......*discuss*...... the book we read in class.
2 I don't understand this exercise. Can you ....
it to me, please?
3 I don't like going to football matches because everybody .... at the players.
4 She doesn't want to go to the show, and there's nothing you can say to .... her.
5 The teacher gets angry if we .... to each other during the lesson.
6 Listen very carefully, because I'm not going to .... what I say.
7 For our English homework, we had to ....
what our bedroom looks like.
8 We .... for an hour about where to go on Saturday, but we couldn't agree.

4 Work in pairs.

- What do you usually chat with your friends about?
- When was the last time you shouted at someone?
- Have you ever explained something to someone else What was it?
- When was the last time someone persuaded you to something you didn't want to?
- What subject do you enjoy discussing the most?

Reading Part 4

- When you have finished, read the whole text again to make sure it makes sense.

Exam advice

1 Look at the adverts. What are they trying to communicate? Which do you think is the best way to advertise something?

2 For each question, choose the correct answer.

SKYWRITING

You don't see much skywriting these days, but many years ago it was a very
(1) .... kind of advertising. Drinks companies and car maker
(2) .... skywriting companies lots of money to get their
messages into the sky.

Skywriting has always been expensive and difficult and you can never
(3) .... what the weather will be like. 'We have to have blue
skies,' says Susan Althrop, who has a skywriting business in France.
'Customers can **(4)** .... a flight for next month, but it might
be cloudy or windy!'

There aren't **(5)** .... skywriters left now. Susan's customers
usually companies looking for an unusual **(6)** .... to adverti
Each job costs around €5,000 – so people have to be quite rich to do it!

	A		B		C	
1	A	popular	B	favourite	C	busy
2	A	made	B	paid	C	bought
3	A	think	B	hope	C	know
4	A	book	B	keep	C	save
5	A	some	B	much	C	many
6	A	way	B	sort	C	type

Grammar

Present perfect with *just*, *already* and *yet*

▶ **Page 131 Grammar reference**
Present perfect with *just*, *already* and *yet*

Have you ever written a letter? Who did you write to?

Look at the pictures below. Then complete the rules with the <u>underlined</u> words.

A Eva has <u>just</u> written a letter.

B Eva has <u>already</u> bought a stamp.

C Eva hasn't posted her letter <u>yet</u>.

Rules

We use ......*already*...... for something that happened before now.

We use .... for something that has not happened, but will soon.

We use .... for something that happened a very short time ago.

③ **Choose the correct words in *italics*.**

1 He's *just / already* fallen in the river.

2 I'm sure we've *yet / already* seen this film.

3 She hasn't finished her project *yet / already*.

4 They've *just / yet* missed the train.

5 I can't believe you've *already / yet* eaten everything!

6 Have you tidied your room *already / yet*?

④ **/P/ Sentence stress**
 Listen and <u>underline</u> the stressed words.

1 I've just finished.
2 I've already done it!
3 I haven't made it yet.

⑤ **Work in pairs. Ask and answer questions with *just*, *already* and *yet*. Use the ideas in the box.**

> build a website   do your homework   go to another country
> have breakfast   learn to drive   win a prize

Have you had breakfast yet?

No, I haven't had breakfast yet.

Vocabulary
-ed / -ing adjectives

1 Look at the photos. How do you think each person feels? Why? Use adjectives from the box.

> bored   excited   interested   surprised   tired   worried

A
B
C
D
E
F

2 Listen to the conversation. Which photo from Exercise 1 is it? *85*

3 Listen again and answer the questions. *85*
1 Who is bored?   2 What is boring?

4 Choose the correct endings in *italics*.

Rules
1 Adjectives ending in *-ed / -ing* describe how we feel.
2 Adjectives ending in *-ed / -ing* describe what makes us feel that way.

5 Listen to the conversations. Complete the sentences with the correct form of adjectives from Exercise 1. *86*
1 The result of the tennis match was ....*surprising*.... Nicky is ....
2 The children are ....
 The long walk is ....
3 Tomorrow's maths exam is .... for Jamie.
 Jamie is .... about it.
4 Today is an .... day for Suzie.
 She's very ....
5 They are .... in the book.
 The book is ....

6 Work in pairs. Imagine you are in these situations. Describe to your partner how you feel, using *-ed* and *-ing* adjectives.
1 Your friend hasn't replied to your message. You don' know what's happened to him.
 It's worrying. I'm worried.
2 You're running in a 10km race and you're near the e You're winning!
3 You are doing an exam at school. The fire alarm go off very loudly.
4 You suddenly get a message on your phone. It's fro Taylor Swift!
5 You are writing a story for English homework. A cat jumps on to your desk.

Reading Part 5

- This part of the exam often includes prepositions.
- When you have filled the gaps, read the text again to make sure it makes sense.
- Always check your spelling!

Exar advic

1 Choose the correct words in *italics*.
1 We're going there *with / by / in* car.
2 I'm going to stay *in / of / at* home tonight.
3 Have you written *at / on / to* your uncle yet?
4 The film starts *at / by / in* half an hour.
5 I'll meet you *at / in / during* 7 o'clock.
6 Dan is leaving *at / in / on* Tuesday.
7 Thank you *of / to / for* talking to me.
8 I have a picture *to / of / in* you on my website.

Work in pairs.

- Have you ever been to a summer camp?
- How do you keep in touch with new friends you make?

keep in touch *(phr)*
to communicate or continue to communicate with someone by phoning, or writing to them

Complete the email. For each question, write the correct answer. Write one word for each gap.

Hi Linn,

It **(0)** ....*was*.......... great to meet you at the summer camp in the UK. I really enjoyed learning more English with you. I've never had so **(1)** .... fun in a class before!

(2) .... is great that our class has a Snapchat group, but I also like writing emails. I wrote **(3)** .... Haru yesterday. He says he's thinking **(4)** .... going to summer camp again next year.

I also sent Beppe a message, but he hasn't written back yet. **(5)** .... you heard from him?

I have to go now. My Spanish class starts **(6)** .... five minutes.

Love, Eva

peaking Parts 1 and 2

▶ **Page 146 Speaking bank**
Speaking Parts 1 and 2

- If you don't understand what your partner (or the examiner) says, say *Can you repeat that, please?* or *Sorry, I didn't understand.*

Exam advice

Look at a student's answers. Write the questions.

1 .... ?
   Monica Reis.

2 .... ?
   I'm 12 years old.

3 .... ?
   I'm from Spain.

4 .... ?
   I live in Madrid.

Listen and check. Then work in pairs and ask and answer the questions.

---

3 The examiner will ask you questions on two topics. Choose two topics and write two questions for each.

food   home   music   school subjects   shopping

4 Work in pairs. Ask and answer your questions.

5 Look at the pictures. What do you think the examiner will ask? Listen and check.

6 Listen again. Then work in pairs and discuss the pictures.

7 Listen to these candidates. Write the missing words.

Examiner: Martin, do you prefer meeting your friends at your home or in a café?

Martin: I like **(1)** .... my friends at my house.

Examiner: Why?

Martin: Sometimes they come to my house and sometimes I go to where they live. In the **(2)** .... it's good because we can **(3)** .... at my friend's house.

Examiner: Mina, is it better to write a message or talk on the phone?

Mina: It's **(4)** .... Sometimes it's better to talk on the phone. But I **(5)** .... send a message on Whatsapp or text my friends. We have a group and we can talk there. But I talk to my **(6)** .... on the phone. That's **(7)** ....

Examiner: Do you prefer **(8)** .... your friends at your home or in a café?

Mina: In a café, usually.

Examiner: Why?

Mina: Because I like to **(9)** .... of the house sometimes. All my friends do, too.

8 Work in pairs. Practise asking and answering the questions from Exercise 7.

13 Vocabulary and grammar review

Grammar

1 Complete the second sentence so that it means the same as the first. Use the present perfect and *for* or *since*.

1 The last time I ate was five hours ago.

I .... *haven't eaten for* .... five hours.

2 We came to live here when I was eight, and we still live here now.

We .... I was eight.

3 Josh met Chloe three months ago.

Josh .... three months.

4 The last time I saw the sea was in 2011.

I .... 2011.

5 My parents bought me this laptop four years ago, and I still have it.

I .... four years.

6 I got to school at eight o'clock this morning, and I'm still here.

I .... eight o'clock this morning.

7 The last time it rained here was two weeks ago.

It .... two weeks.

8 I loved this film when I first saw it and I still love it.

I .... last June.

2 Complete the dialogues with *might* or *might not*.

1 **A:** I called Maria twice, but she didn't answer.
B: She ..... *might not* ..... have her mobile phone with her.

2 **A:** What are you doing tonight?
B: I don't know. I .... stay in and play computer games.

3 **A:** I'll be so happy when I win this race.
B: But you .... win!

4 **A:** What are you going to wear to Marta's fancy dress party?
B: I .... go as a pirate.

5 **A:** Let's buy a classical music CD for John.
B: But he .... like classical music.

6 **A:** How are you getting to the station tomorrow?
B: I .... walk.

7 **A:** Shall we go to Simon's house?
B: Yes, but let's call him first. He .... be at home.

8 **A:** I'm going to lie in the sun all day when I'm on holiday in Spain.
B: It .... be sunny when you're there.

Vocabulary

3 Complete the definitions, then find the words in the puzzle.

1 A .... *coach* .... teaches people how to do a sport.
2 A .... fixes cars.
3 A .... writes and reports the news.
4 A .... helps the doctors in a hospital.
5 A .... uses a camera.
6 A .... is a doctor for animals.
7 A .... flies planes.

P	H	O	T	O	G	R	A	P	H	E
D	O	C	B	E	N	S	W	E	T	U
G	C	V	E	T	U	P	P	C	L	R
J	O	U	R	N	A	L	I	S	T	S
I	A	E	W	K	T	E	L	A	C	E
B	C	E	A	L	E	W	O	N	M	X
C	H	E	V	N	E	R	T	I	M	C
F	D	M	E	C	H	A	N	I	C	M
R	T	O	T	R	G	U	I	D	E	G

4 Complete the sentences with the adverb form of the underlined adjectives.

1 My mum is a <u>wonderful</u> singer. She sings *wonderf[...]*
2 Fred is a <u>good</u> driver. He drives ....
3 I'm a <u>bad</u> singer. I sing ....
4 You're a really <u>slow</u> walker. You walk really ....
5 Dogs are <u>fast</u> runners. They run ....
6 Tina is a <u>careful</u> cyclist. She cycles ....
7 This is an <u>easy</u> exercise. I can do it ....
8 This baby has a <u>happy</u> laugh. He laughs ....

Grammar

Complete the sentences with the past participle of the verbs in the box.

> build   ~~clean~~   cook   give   hurt   invite

1 You'll be in trouble if this room isn't ......*cleaned*...... by the time I get home!
2 I think this chicken was .... for too long.
3 How many parties are you .... to every year?
4 Do you know when this school was ....?
5 We weren't .... enough time to finish the test.
6 There was an accident here yesterday, but fortunately nobody was ....

Change the sentences into the passive.

1 Lots of tourists visit this city.
   This city is visited by lots of tourists.
2 My grandfather painted this picture.
   ....
3 Our teacher wrote this book.
   ....
4 Italians make good pizzas.
   ....
5 Nobody heard the noise.
   ....
6 My friends laughed at me.
   ....
7 Everybody loves you!
   ....

Choose the correct words in *italics* to complete the conversation.

Patrick: Hi, Sam. Have you finished your homework **(1)** *just* / (*yet*)?

Sam: No. I've **(2)** *just* / *already* started it. It looks really hard.

Patrick: It isn't. It's easy. I've finished mine **(3)** *already* / *yet*! Listen, do you want to come to the cinema? I've **(4)** *just* / *yet* heard the new Disney film is on.

Sam: No thanks, I've **(5)** *yet* / *already* seen it.

Patrick: Oh, well come out anyway. We could go to the new café that's **(6)** *just* / *yet* opened on Queen Street.

Sam: I can't.

Patrick: Why not?

Sam: I told you – I haven't finished my homework **(7)** *already* / *yet*.

Vocabulary

④ Choose the correct option, A, B or C.

1 Let's have a meeting to ....*discuss*....... our holiday plans.
   A chat   **B discuss**   C repeat
2 If you don't understand the question, ask the examiner to .... it.
   A describe   B shout   **C repeat**
3 We can't hear you at the back of the room. You'll have to ....
   A shout   B chat   C ask
4 I'll .... Stefan if he wants to come with us.
   A explain   B ask   C discuss
5 Can you .... the man who stole your bicycle?
   A explain   B chat   C describe
6 It's very hard to .... the problem.
   A repeat   B explain   C shout
7 She spends a lot of time .... with her friends on her mobile.
   A chatting   B explaining   C discussing

⑤ Complete the sentences with words from the box.

> ~~excited~~   exciting   interested   interesting
> surprised   surprising   tired   tiring

1 We're really ....*excited*....... about starting our new school.
2 That was the most .... film I've ever seen.
3 This book isn't very ....
4 Are you .... in computers?
5 I don't like running. It's really ....
6 You should go to bed if you're ....
7 Mark was very .... to see us.
8 I didn't think that was going to happen! That was ....

Grammar reference

1

PRESENT SIMPLE

be

Positive/Negative forms

I	am/'m	
	am not/'m not	13 years old. Spanish. happy.
You/We/They	are/'re	
	are not/aren't	
He/She/It	is/'s	
	is not/isn't	

Question forms

Am	I	
Are	you/we/they	13 years old? Spanish?
Is	he/she/it	

Short answers

	I	am.
Yes,	he/she/it	is.
	we/they	are.
	I	am not.
No,	he/she/it	isn't.
	we/they	aren't.

We use *be* to talk about:
- nationality: *I'm French.*
- age: *She's 14.*
- jobs: *My mum and dad are teachers.*
- feelings: ***Are** you happy?*
- time: *It's 10 o'clock.*
- where things are: The plates **are** on the table.

PRACTICE

1 Rewrite each sentence with the short forms of the underlined words.

1 <u>You are</u> 16 years old. ......*You're*......

2 My brother <u>is not</u> very funny. ....

3 **A:** Are you French?
   B: No, <u>I am not</u> ....

4 We <u>are not</u> teachers. <u>We are</u> students. ....

5 <u>She is</u> Australian. ....

2 Complete each sentence with the correct form of be.

1 My sister .... 19.

2 I .... not very happy this morning.

3 Two of my friends .... American.

4 **A:** .... your mother a doctor?
   B: No, she .... She .... a teacher.

5 **A:** .... you 12 years old?
   B: Yes, I ....

OTHER VERBS

We use present simple verbs to talk about:

- things that happen regularly: *We **go** to school every day.*
- things that are always true: *Summer **comes** after spring. We **live** in Paris.*

Positive/Negative forms

I/You/We/They	like	
	don't like	chocolate.
He/She/It	likes	
	doesn't like	

Question forms

Do	you/we/they	like chocolate?
Does	he/she/it	

Short answers

Yes,	I/we/they	do.
	he/she/it	does.
No,	I/we/they	don't.
	he/she/it	doesn't.

The he/she/it form of most verbs uses the infinitive + -s.
Sometimes we add -es (do > does; go > goes).
If the verb ends in a -y, we add -ies (carry > carries).

PRACTICE

Complete each sentence with the correct form of the verb in brackets.

Paul .... the piano every evening. (play)

I .... at 6 o'clock every day. (get up)

My brother .... football. (like)

My friends .... near me. (live)

Hannah .... to school by bus. (go)

Write the negative form of the sentences from Exercise 3.

Paul ....

I ....

My brother ....

My friends ....

Hannah ....

Underline and correct the mistake in each sentence.

My father work in London.

Tom don't play the piano.

I plays football every weekend.

Does she starts work at 9 o'clock every morning?

My parents doesn't watch TV in the afternoon.

ADVERBS OF FREQUENCY

Frequency adverbs tell us how often something happens.

always		I **always** go to bed at night.
usually		I **usually** go to bed at 10.00.
often		I **often** go to bed at 11.00.
sometimes		I **sometimes** go to bed at midnight.
never		I **never** go to bed at lunchtime.

- We use frequency adverbs after the verb *be*:
  They **are always** happy at the weekend.
- We usually put frequency adverbs before other verbs:
  I **often get** home at 5 o'clock.
  In negative sentences, frequency adverbs come between *don't/doesn't* and the verb:
  We **don't always get up** early at the weekend.
  We can also use expressions like *every day, twice a week, once a year* to say how often something happens. We put these at the beginning or the end of sentences.
  Every year, we go on holiday to Italy.
  I have piano lessons **once a week**.

PRACTICE

6 Put the words in order to make sentences.

1 evening. / go / I / in / never / school / the / to

2 help / homework. / me / My /my / parents / sometimes / with

3 and / I / brother / day / every / My / school. / to / walk

4 am / for / I / late / school. / sometimes

5 always / at / hard / I / school. / work

7 Make these sentences true for you. Add adverbs or other frequency expressions.

1 get up at 7 o'clock in the morning

....

....

2 have lunch at school

....

....

3 go out in the evening

....

....

4 go to bed at 10 o'clock

....

....

5 sleep for eight hours

....

....

2

PRESENT CONTINUOUS

Positive/Negative forms

I	am/'m	eating.
	am not/'m not	
You/We/They	are/'re	
	are not/aren't	
He/She/It	is/'s	
	is not/isn't	

Question forms

Am	I	eating?
Are	you/we/they	
Is	he/she/it	

Short answers

Yes,	I	am.
	he/she/it	is.
	we/they	are.
No,	I	am not.
	he/she/it	isn't.
	we/they	aren't.

We use present continuous verbs to talk about things that are happening now:
I'm watching a film on TV.

Spelling

Most verbs	add *-ing* to the infinitive	watch – **watching** find – **finding**
Verbs ending in *-e*	take off *-e*, then add *-ing*	like – **liking** write – **writing**
Verbs with one syllable, ending in one vowel and one consonant	repeat the last consonant and add *-ing*	put – **putting** run – **running**

PRACTICE

1 Complete the sentences with the present continuous fo of the verbs in brackets.

1 My parents .... (not watch) TV. They .... (listen) to music.

2 I .... (write) an email to my cousin in France

3 **A:** .... (you, do) your homework?
B: No, I .... (not). I .... (play) a computer game.

4 Tom .... (run) to school because he's late.

5 Maria .... (not wash) her hair.

2 Underline and correct the spelling mistake in each sentence.

1 Ben is readding one of his school books.

2 Emma and Anna are puting their clothes away.

3 Are you cookeing our lunch?

4 I'm siting in the kitchen.

5 My brother and sister are danceing in the garden.

AVE GOT

Positive/Negative forms

I/You/We/They	have got	
	haven't got	a phone.
He/She	has got	
	hasn't got	

Question forms

Have	you/we/they	
Has	he/she/it	got a phone?

Short answers

Yes,	I/we/they	have.
	he/she/it	has.
No,	I/we/they	haven't.
	he/she/it	hasn't.

short answers we do not use *got*.
I **have**. ~~Yes, I have got.~~

have got to talk about:

hings we own:
ve got a new smartphone.
ow people look.
he's **got** blue eyes.
eople in our families.
have got two brothers and a sister.

PRACTICE

3 **Choose the correct words in** *italics*.

1 Kelly *hasn't / haven't* got any shoes to wear for the party.

2 Paul and Liza *has / have* got two children.

3 My brother and I *has / have* got black hair.

4 **A:** *Has / Have* we got any homework tonight?
  B: No, we *hasn't / haven't*.

5 All my friends *has / have* got smartphones.

4 **Complete each sentence with the correct form of have got.**

1 My family is very large. I .... three brothers and two sisters.

2 We don't know what the time because we .... a watch.

3 My older brother Ben .... a new car.

4 **A:** I don't know where my phone is. .... you .... it?

  B: No, I ....

5 I'm sorry, but we .... any coffee.

3

COUNTABLE AND UNCOUNTABLE NOUNS

Countable nouns	Uncountable nouns
• are things we can count: a **school**, two **teachers**, three **students**	• are things we cannot count: **air**, **milk**, **money**
• can be singular or plural: one **student**, two **students**	• can't be plural ~~airs, milks or informations~~
• take *a*, *an* or numbers I am a **student**. I have **three teachers**.	• do not go after *a*, *an* or numbers: I like **water**. I like ~~a water~~.

some and *any*

Use *some*	Use *any*
• with plural countable nouns: **Some students** are talking an exam today. • with uncountable nouns in affirmative sentences: I've got **some money** in my pocket. • in offers or requests: Would you like **some** coffee? Can you lend me **some** money, please?	• with plural nouns in negative sentences and questions: We haven't got **any books** with us. Have you got **any questions**? • and uncountable nouns in negative sentences and questions: She has**n't** got **any money**. Do we have **any coffee**?

Plural forms	
For most nouns, add -s	student – **students** banana – **bananas**
For nouns which end in -s, -ch, -sh, -x, add -es	bus – **buses** match – **matches** dish – **dishes** box – **boxes**
For some nouns which end in -f or -fe, change -f to -v and add -es	half – **halves** knife – **knives** wife – **wives**
For nouns which end in consonant + -y, change the -y to -ies	family – **families** city – **cities**
Some nouns are irregular.	child – **children** man – **men** woman – **women** person – **people**

ACTICE

Complete the table with nouns from the box.

baby box bread child coffee juice knife man
milk money person rice school strawberry
student tea teacher water

Countable nouns	Uncountable nouns
baby	

Write the plural forms of the countable nouns in Exercise 1.

aby ....*babies*.......

omplete the sentences with a, an, some or any.

Would you like .... apple?

Do we need .... vegetables?

.... students are not at school today.

Please can I have .... water?

We haven't got .... coffee.

There's .... phone on the floor.

W MUCH /MANY; A FEW, A LITTLE, OT OF

se these words and phrases to talk about quantity.

e **How much** with uncountable nouns.
w much money have you got?
w much food do we need for our party?
e **How many** with plural countable nouns.
w many students are in your class?
w many people are coming to our party?
e **a little** (= not much) with uncountable nouns.
n I borrow **a little sugar**, please?
ere's still **a little time** left.
e **a few** (= not many) with plural countable nouns.
n I borrow **a few cups**, please?
ere are **a few good films** on TV tonight.

• Use **a lot of** (= a large number) with plural countable nouns and uncountable nouns.
There are **a lot of people** in the supermarket.
We've got **a lot of money** in the bank.
• Use **no** (= not any) with plural countable nouns and uncountable nouns.
There are **no vegetables** in the kitchen.
There's **no milk** in the fridge.

PRACTICE

④ **Choose the correct words in *italics*.**

A: **(1)** *How much / How many* food do we need for the party?
B: I'm not sure. **(2)** *How much / How many* people are coming?
A: **(3)** *A lot of / A little* adults and **(4)** *a little / a few* children.
B: OK, so we need **(5)** *a lot of / a few* food. And drinks?
A: We have **(6)** *no / a little* drinks at the moment.
B: OK. Let's get **(7)** *a few / a little* orange juice for the children and **(8)** *a few / a little* other things for the adults.

4

PRESENT CONTINUOUS AND PRESENT SIMPLE

We use the present continuous to talk about things that are happening now:
We're watching television at the moment.

We use the present simple:

- to talk about things we do regularly.
  I usually **watch** television in the evening.
  I **walk** to school.
- with verbs that describe states (things that don't change)
  be, **like**, **hate**, **have**, **want**, **love**, **know**, **understand**.
  I **like** tea but I **hate** coffee.
  I **have** three brothers, and I **love** them all.

- We do not usually use state verbs in the present continuous.
  I **understand** German and Spanish.
  ~~I am understanding~~ German and Spanish.
- The verb *have* is a state verb when we talk about things that don't change.
  I **have** two brothers.
- We can use the continuous form of *have* for actions:
  We're **having** breakfast.
  He's **having** a wash.

PRACTICE

1 **Choose the correct words in *italics*.**

1 My brother and I *go / are going* to school by bus every day.

2 Dan can't come out. He *does / is doing* his homework.

3 I *love / am loving* school holidays.

4 Oh no! It *starts / is starting* to rain.

5 My sister and I *play / are playing* tennis every Saturday.

6 In our family, we *have / are having* a dog and three cats.

2 **<u>Underline</u> and correct the mistake in each sentence.**

1 After school, we are usually getting home at five o'clock.

2 Ssh! I listen to the news on the radio.

3 Everyone in my family is hating cold weather.

4 Ben is having a brother and a sister.

5 Jon has a shower at the moment.

6 Am I talking too quickly? Are you understanding me?

TOO AND ENOUGH

- *too* + adjective means 'more than we need' or 'more than is possible'.
  This food is **too hot**. (I don't like it, or I can't eat it.)
  I'm not going swimming because the water is too cold.
  (= I would like warmer water.)
- *not* + adjective + enough means 'less than we need' or 'less than is possible'.
  I'm **not warm enough**. (= I'm cold. I want to be warmer.)
  This T-shirt is **not big enough** for me. (= I am bigger than the T-shirt.)

- We can also use *not enough* + plural countable noun or uncountable noun.
  There **aren't enough drinks** for everyone.
  We **don't have enough money** for a new car.
  Notice the correct word order: *I'm not **warm enough**. (~~I'~~ ~~enough warm.~~)*
  We don't have **enough money**. (~~We don't have money en~~

PRACTICE

3 **Rewrite these sentences using not enough + the adje in brackets.**

1 My bike is too slow. (fast) .... *My bike isn't fast eno...*

2 Tom's coat is too small. (big) ....

3 This exercise is too hard. (easy) ....

4 My tea is too cold. (hot) ....

5 I'm too young to drive. (old) ....

6 Those jeans are too expensive for me. (cheap) ....

4 **Rewrite these sentences using too + the adjective in brackets.**

1 The sea isn't warm enough for a swim. (cold)
....

2 That bag isn't light enough for me. (heavy)
....

3 Those plates aren't clean enough. (dirty)
....

4 My computer isn't fast enough. (slow)
....

5 I'm not tall enough for basketball. (short)
....

OMPARATIVES AND SUPERLATIVES

use comparative adjectives to talk about the difference
ween two people or things.
*nah is **younger** than her sister.*
*n **taller** than my best friend.*

superlative adjectives to talk about the difference between
ee or more people or things.
*nah is the **youngest** child in the family.*

adjective	comparative	superlative
one syllable (e.g. *small*), add *-er* or *-est*	**smaller**, **colder** than	the **smallest**, the **coldest**
one syllable ending in *-e* (e.g. *large*, *nice*), add *-r* or *-est*	**larger**, **nicer** than	the **largest**, the **nicest**
short adjectives ending in vowel + consonant (e.g. *big*, *thin*), double the consonant and add *-er* or *-est*	**bigger**, **thinner** than	the **biggest**, the **thinnest**
ending in *-y* (e.g. *heavy*, *pretty*), take off the *-y* and add *-ier* or *-iest*	**heavier**, **prettier** than	the **heaviest**, the **prettiest**
with three syllables or more (e.g. *difficult*, *important*), add *more* or *most*	**more difficult**, **more important** than	the **most difficult** the **most important**
irregular adjectives (e.g. *good*, *bad*)	**better**, **worse** than	the **best**, the **worst**

PRACTICE

1 Complete the sentences with the comparative form of the
adjectives in brackets.

1 My class is .... than my brother's class. (big)

2 Today's homework is .... than yesterday's
   homework. (interesting)

3 My new bike is .... than my old one. (heavy)

4 The sea is .... than it was last week. (warm)

5 The weather today is .... than it was
   yesterday. (bad)

6 These shoes are too small. I need .... ones
   (large).

2 Underline and correct the mistake in each sentence.

1 I am the better footballer in my class.

2 Anna is happyer than she was this morning.

3 I want to be fiter so I do lots of exercise.

4 What is the more expensive thing you have?

5 Ben's apartment is largerer than mine.

6 Tom is taller his father.

the tallest student in the class.

e often use *than* after comparative adjectives: *I am*
unger than her.
e often use *the* before superlative adjectives: *She is **the***
*ungest** person in the family.*
e often use phrases like these after superlative adjectives:
the family, in the world, in the class (NOT ~~of the family~~, ~~of~~
~~e world~~, ~~of the class~~).

PREPOSITIONS OF TIME: *AT, IN, ON*

We use *at*, *in* and *on* when we talk about time.

at	clock times	*I get up **at six o'clock**.* *I have lunch **at midday**.*
	some festivals	*We have parties **at New Year**.*
	meal times	***At lunchtime**, we sometimes go to the café.*
	with weekend and night	*What do you do **at the weekend**?* *I often work **at night**.*
	other phrases	*I'm studying **at the moment**.*
in	parts of the day	*I go to school **in the morning** and come home **in the evening**.*
	months, seasons	*My birthday is **in May**.* *We go on holiday **in summer**.*
	years	*I was born **in 2002** and started school **in 2007**.*
	other phrases	*I did my homework **in** two hours.*
on	weekdays	*I play football **on Saturdays**.* *Let's meet **on Monday evening**.*
	dates	*The match is **on 3 April**.* *School starts **on 4 September**.*

PRACTICE

3 **Complete each sentence with *at*, *in* or *on*.**

1 We don't go to school .... Sundays.

2 I always go shopping .... the weekend.

3 Our holiday starts .... 23 December.

4 I do my homework .... the evening.

5 My sister's birthday is .... February.

6 I usually wake up .... 7 o'clock.

4 **Underline and correct the mistake in each sentence.**

1 We often go swimming in Tuesday evenings.

2 We always have a big party on the end of the year.

3 My younger brother was born on 2013.

4 What do you eat in breakfast time?

5 Let's meet on the afternoon tomorrow.

6 I don't like working in night.

AVE TO

We use *have/has to* + infinitive to talk about things that are necessary:
I **have to go** to school five days a week.

We use *don't have/doesn't have to* + infinitive to talk about things that are not necessary:
I **don't have to go** to school at the weekend.

Positive/Negative forms

I/You/We/They	**have to**	go to school tomorrow.
	don't have to	
He/She/It	**has to**	
	doesn't have to	

Question forms

Do	you/we/they	**have to** go to school tomorrow?
Does	he/she	

Short answers

Yes,	I/we/they	**do**.
	he/she/it	**does**.
No,	I/we/they	**don't**.
	he/she/it	**doesn't**.

Complete the conversation with the correct form of *have to* and the verbs in brackets.

Hi. Do you want to go swimming?

No, I can't. My sister and I **(1)** .... (help) our parents.

What **(2)** .... (you do)?

To start with I **(3)** .... (tidy) my bedroom.

And your sister? **(4)** .... (tidy) her bedroom, too?

Yes, **(5)** ...., and then she **(6)** .... (wash) the car. And you?

I **(7)** .... (not do) anything!

Choose the correct verbs in *italics*.

Teachers *have to / don't have to* work in schools.

Students *have to / don't have to* go to school in the holidays.

Young children *have to / don't have to* go to work every day.

Farmers *have to / don't have to* work outside.

Police officers *have to / don't have to* wear uniforms.

OBJECT PRONOUNS

subject pronoun	object pronoun
I	**me**
you	**you**
he	**him**
she	**her**
it	**it**
we	**us**
they	**them**

- In most sentences, subject pronouns go before the main verb. Object pronouns go after the main verb. (The underlined words in these sentences are subject pronouns. The **bold** words are object pronouns.)
She likes **you**.
We are watching **them**.

- We can use object pronouns instead of a noun when we don't want to repeat the noun.
*My **teacher** is Mr. André. I like **him**.*

- Object pronouns can also come after prepositions.
*He's reading **to them**.*
*The teacher is talking **to us**.*

PRACTICE

3 Rewrite the sentences, starting with the word given. Do not change the meaning.

1 I like her. She .... *likes me* ....

2 He's phoning her.
She's ....

3 We go to school with them.
They ....

4 They're watching me.
I'm ....

5 You're reading to him.
He's ....

6 She's helping me.
I'm ....

4 Complete these sentences with pronouns.

1 I have two sisters. I like .... very much.

2 My brother is in a different class to me, but I go to school with .... every day.

3 My mother is always busy. I help .... when I can.

4 Ben and I are with some friends. .... are playing football with ....

5 Mr. Holmes is eating his lunch. .... is really enjoying ....

7

PAST SIMPLE

be

Positive/Negative forms

I/He/She/It	**was**	at home yesterday.
	was not/wasn't	
You/We/They	**were**	
	were not/weren't	

Question forms

Was	I/he/she/it	at home yesterday?
Were	you/we/they	

Short answers

Yes,	I he/she/it	**was.**
	we/they	**were.**
No,	I he/she/it	**wasn't.**
	we/they	**weren't.**

We use *was/were* to talk about the past:
*We **were** at school yesterday. Our new teacher **was** very interesting.*

Other verbs

Positive/Negative forms

I/He/She/You/We/They	**enjoyed**	the film last night.
	did not/didn't enjoy	

Question forms

Did	you/we/they he/she/it	**enjoy** the film**?**

Short answers

Yes,	I/we/they	**did.**
No,	he/she/it	**didn't.**

We use the past simple to talk about finished events in the past:
*We **studied** a lot today.*
*I **watched** TV last night.*

We often use time expressions with past simple verbs, for example, *last year, yesterday, a week ago.*

Spelling of past simple regular verbs

Most verbs	add -*ed*	*watch* – **watched**
Verbs ending in -*e*	add -*d*	*like* – **liked**
Verbs with one syllable, ending in one vowel and one consonant	repeat the last consonant and add -*ed*	*stop* – **stopped**
Verb ending in a consonant + -*y*	change -*y* to -*i* and add -*ed*	*study* – **studied**

Irregular verbs

There are many irregular past simple verbs in English. Here some common ones.

present simple	past simple
break	**broke**
come	**came**
do	**did**
drink	**drank**
eat	**ate**
get	**got**
give	**gave**
go	**went**
have	**had**
leave	**left**
see	**saw**
take	**took**

*We **left** home at 8.30.*
*We **went** on holiday to France last year.*

ACTICE

Complete the short conversations with the past simple form of the verbs in brackets.

1 A: Why .... (be) you late for school yesterday?
  B: Our bus .... (break) down, so we .... (walk).

2 A: What .... you .... (have) for breakfast this morning?
  B: I .... (eat) toast and eggs and I .... (drink) orange juice.

3 A: What .... you .... (get) for your birthday?
  B: I .... (get) a new phone from my parents and my sister .... (give) me a T-shirt.

  A: .... you .... (go) out yesterday?
  B: Yes, we .... (do). We .... (go) to a club.

  A: .... you .... (watch) the football match on TV?
  B: No, I .... (do not). My dad .... (take) me to the game. It .... (be) great!

  A: I .... (come) to see you this morning, but you .... (not be) in.
  B: Sorry, I .... (be) at the dentist.

Complete these sentences with the past simple form of the regular verbs in the box.

> begin   buy   feel   leave   make   meet   win

We .... home this morning at 7.30.

I .... two races at the weekend but I .... very tired afterwards.

My brother and I .... lunch for the whole family yesterday.

I .... my friends in town on Saturday. We .... some new clothes.

I .... to do my homework at seven o'clock. That was three hours ago.

IMPERATIVES

We use the imperative form when we tell someone to do something or not to do something.

Positive sentences

Turn to page 50.
Be quick!

Negative sentences

Don't be late!
Don't eat so quickly.

We can make imperatives sound more polite by adding *please*.
Turn to page 50, **please**.
Please don't eat so quickly.

We do not use subject pronouns with imperatives
Get up! (not ~~You get up!~~)
Don't be late! (not ~~Don't you be late!~~)

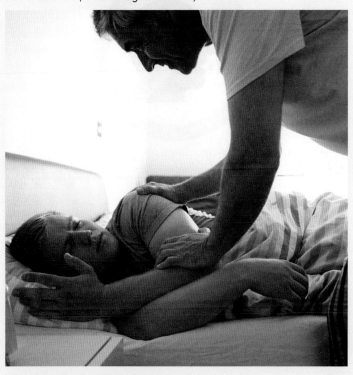

We also use imperatives for:

- instructions or directions.
  Boil a litre of water.
  Turn left at the end of the road.

- advice.
  Rest as much as possible.
  Don't worry!

- orders or warnings.
  Be quiet!
  Don't touch that!

- requests.
  Please **close** the door quietly.

- invitations.
  Come to my party!

3 Complete the sentences with the correct form of the verbs in brackets.

1 .... your phone here. (use)

2 .... here. (shout) .... quietly. (talk)

3 .... here. (run) .... slowly. (walk)

4 .... in here. (come) .... the other door. (use)

4 Write sentences with imperatives. Use verbs from the bo and the words in brackets.

| ~~buy~~ forget go turn wash |

1 These jeans are too small for me. (some new ones)
  ..*Buy some new ones*...

2 My hands are very dirty. (them)

  ....

3 It's Mum's birthday at the weekend.
  (to buy her a present)

  ....

4 The radio is really loud. (it off)

  ....

5 I'm really tired. (to bed)

  ....

AST CONTINUOUS

ositive/Negative forms

I/He/She/It	was	
	was not/wasn't	**listening** to music.
You/We/They	were	
	were not/weren't	

estion forms

Was	I/he/she/it	**listening** to music?
Were	you/we/they	

ort answers

Yes,	I	**was.**
	he/she/it	
	we/they	**were.**
No,	I	**wasn't.**
	he/she/it	
	we/they	**weren't.**

use the past continuous:
> talk about something happening over a period of time in
he past.
/e **were watching** a film at 8 o'clock last night.
> talk about two things happening at the same time:
hey **were watching** the film while I **was doing** my
omework.
ith the past simple to talk about one thing happening in
he middle of another.
hen I left home, my brother **was eating** his breakfast.
hile I **was walking** into town, it started to rain.

We use *while* to talk about two continuous actions.
I **was doing** my homework **while** my parents **were watching** TV.

We use *when* to talk about a point of time.
My parents **were watching** TV **when** I got home.

PRACTICE

1 Choose the correct verbs in italics.

1 While *we had / were having* lunch, *we listened / were listening* to the news.

2 I *slept / was sleeping* when you *phoned / were phoning* this morning.

3 At 3 o'clock this afternoon I *did / was doing* a maths test at school.

4 When I *woke up / was waking up* this morning, it *rained / was raining*.

5 What *are you doing / were you doing* at 10 o'clock last night?

2 Complete the story with past forms of verbs from this list. You need eight past continuous verbs and two past simple verbs.

> be   come   ~~drive~~   listen   read   see   stand   stop
> tell   travel

It was a sunny morning and my parents, my sister and I (1) *were driving* along a busy motorway. We (2) .... to Scotland to spend the weekend with some family friends. My sister and I (3) .... magazines and Mum and Dad (4) .... to music on the car radio. Suddenly we (5) .... bright blue lights on the road in front of us. A policeman in a yellow jacket (6) .... in the middle of the road. He (7) .... everyone to drive more slowly. After a few minutes we (8) .... the car. There were two fire engines at the side of the road near to a burning car. Smoke (9) .... out of its engine. Luckily, no-one (10) .... hurt.

CAN, CAN'T, COULD/COULDN'T + INFINITIVE WITHOUT *TO*

We use *can/can't* to talk about present abilities.
I **can play** the piano.
I **can't play** the guitar.
Can you speak French?
Yes, I **can**. / *No, I* **can't**.

We use *could/couldn't* to talk about past abilities.
My sister **could talk** *before she* **could walk**.
I **couldn't sleep** last night.
Could you hear what I said?
Yes, I **could**. / *No, I* **couldn't**.

The infinitive without *to* follows *can/can't* and *could/couldn't*.

The forms of *can, can't, could, couldn't* do not change.

I can (not ~~cans~~) *cook*.

PRACTICE

3 Complete each sentence with *can/can't* or *could/couldn't*

1 I've broken my arm, so I .... play tennis at th
moment.

2 Some babies .... swim before they
.... walk.

3 I .... hear what you're saying. The music is t
loud.

4 My mother says I .... walk when I was one y
old, but I .... when I was two.

5 **A:** .... you cook?
   B: No, I ....

4 Write questions starting with can or could and then giv
short answers that are true for you.

1 ride a bike when you were five?
Could you ride a bike when you were five?
Yes, I could.

2 swim when you were three?
....
....

3 speak more than two languages?
....
....

4 play basketball?
....
....

5 both of your parents drive?
....
....

ING OR TO INFINITIVE AFTER VERBS, ADJECTIVES AND PREPOSITIONS

We use to-infinitive after:

some verbs	choose, help, hope, learn, offer, want	I **hope to go** to university next year. He **wants to help** me. I'm **learning to speak** Italian.
adjectives	happy, difficult, etc.	They were **happy to see** me. This exercise isn't **difficult to do**. She was **surprised to hear** I was ill.
would like, etc.	would like/love/ hate, …	We'**d like to come** and see you later.

We use the -ing form after:

some verbs	enjoy, finish, keep, mind, miss	I **enjoy watching** all sports. We **finished doing** our homework. I **miss seeing** my friends.
prepositions	for, of, about, …	Thanks **for helping** me.

PRACTICE

1 Choose the correct words in italics.

1 I'm pleased *to tell / telling* you the first prize is yours.
2 My dad offered *to help / helping* me with my homework.
3 I enjoy *to play / playing* the piano.
4 Let's finish *to watch / watching* the film before we go to bed.
5 My brother and I enjoy *to play / playing* video games.
6 Thank you for *to help / helping* me.

2 Underline and correct the mistake in each sentence.

1 My friends and I always enjoy to meet in town on Saturdays.
2 I hope visiting Brazil one day.
3 I'm sorry hearing you're ill
4 All my friends enjoy watch football.
5 Do you mind to wait a little longer?

THE FUTURE

WILL

We can use *will/won't* + infinitive without *to* when we talk about the future.

Positive/Negative forms

I/You/He/She/We/They	**will/'ll** **will not/won't**	see you tomorrow.

Question forms

Will	I/you/he/she/we/they	see Ben tomorrow**?**

Short answers

Yes,	I/you/he/she/we/they	**will.**
No,		**won't.**

We can use *will/won't* with these words and phrases.
- *I think/I don't think:*
  I **don't think** Brazil **will** win the match.
- *sure*
  I'm **sure** you'**ll** pass the English test.
- *maybe/probably/perhaps:*
  Maybe they'**ll** be late for the party.
  I'**ll probably** go to bed quite late tonight.
  Perhaps we'll have picnic at the weekend.

We can use *will/won't*:
- to talk about things in the future.
  I think **it will be** warm and sunny tomorrow.
  I'm sure **it won't be** cold and rainy.
- for something we decide at the time of speaking.
  A: *The phone's ringing.*
  B: *I'**ll** answer it.*

PRACTICE

3 Complete the sentences with will or won't and the verbs in brackets.

1 We .... (not have) time to go shopping before we leave.

2 There's someone at the door. I .... (go) and see who it is.

3 **A:** .... you .... (be) away long?
  B: No, I ....

4 I probably .... (not pass) the maths test. I think it .... (be) really difficult.

5 I'm sure we .... (meet) again soon.

4 Put the words in order to make sentences.

1 for / go / holiday / next / our / probably / Spain / to / We / year.

....

2 be / colder / I / it / think / tomorrow. / will

....

3 a / have / new / next / Perhaps / teacher / term. / we'll

....

4 Are / be / OK / sure / you / you'll / ?

....

5 come / He / our / party. / probably / to / won't

....

PRESENT CONTINUOUS FOR THE FUTURE

We can use the present continuous to talk about things happening now. We can also use it to talk about future arrangements:
*My parents **are picking** me **up** from the station tomorrow afternoon.*
*We'**re having** a holiday in Florida next year.*
*I'**m seeing** the doctor later this morning.*

We use *going to* and the present continuous to talk about th[e] future in different ways. We use *going to* when we talk abou[t] something we have decided:
*I'**m going** to have a shower tonight.*

We use the present continuous when we have an arrangem[ent] often with other people:
*I'**m meeting** my friends at the cinema tonight.*

PRESENT SIMPLE FOR THE FUTURE

We can use the present simple to talk about timetabled eve[nts]
*The shop **closes** at 5 pm.*
*The train **leaves** at 2.45.*
*The film **starts** in 10 minutes.*

Positive/Negative forms

I	am/'m am not/'m not	
He/She	is/'s is not/isn't	going to watch TV all evening.
You/We/They	are/'re are not/aren't	

Question forms

Am	I	
Is	he/she	going to stay in tonight?
Are	you/we/they	

Short answers

	I	am.
Yes,	he/she/it	is.
	we/they	are.
	I	'm not.
No,	he/she/it	isn't.
	we/they	aren't.

going to + infinitive to talk about
future plans:
I'm going to spend all evening on my homework.
I'm not going to fall asleep.
things we predict because of something we can see or
because of information we have now:
My older sister is going to have a baby.
It's going to rain. Look at those dark clouds.

PRACTICE

1 Complete the sentences with going to and a verb from the box. There is one verb you do not need to use.

> do   miss   (not) need   phone   ride   visit

1 It's nearly 8 o'clock. You .... your bus.

2 Tomorrow morning, we .... our bikes to school.

3 I .... more exercise in future.

4 We .... our coats. The sun is coming out.

5 We .... our grandparents at the weekend.

2 Complete the conversations with going to.

1 A: You / have coffee for breakfast?
  Are you going to have coffee for breakfast?
  B: No / tea.
  No, I'm going to have tea.

2 A: What you / do this evening?
  ....

  B: I / play a video game.
  ....

3 A: It rain tomorrow?
  ....

  B: No. Look at the red sky. It / sunny all day.
  ....

4 A: What you / do when you leave school?
  ....

  B: I / look for a good job.
  ....

5 A: your team / win the match?
  ....

  B: No, the other team is much better. We / lose.
  ....

PRACTICE

3 Choose the best verb form in italics.

1 From now on, I'm *going to eat / eating* less fast food.

2 We're *going to catch / catching* the 8.40 train tomorrow. I have the tickets.

3 I've got toothache, so I'm *going to see / seeing* the dentist at 9.10 tomorrow.

4 A: What are you *going to do / doing* when you get home?
  B: I'm *going to phone / phoning* my friend.

5 We're *going to have / having* a party on Sunday. It starts at 7.30.

MUST / MUSTN'T

Use *must/mustn't* + infinitive without *to*
- to talk about something that is important and when there is no choice:
  We **must be** at school by 8.30 every morning.
  We **mustn't be** late.
- to give strong advice:
  You **must be** careful when you cross the road.
  You **mustn't cross** without looking.

- *Must* does not change its form.

I/You/He/She/We/They	**must wear** a uniform for school.
	mustn't be late for school.

- We do not usually use *must* in questions. We use *have to*:
  What time **do we have to** be at school?
  Do you have to wear a uniform for school?
- To talk about the past, use *had to*:
  We **had to be** at school at 7.30 yesterday.
  We **had to take** an exam.

PRACTICE

④ **Complete the sentences with *must/mustn't* and verbs fr the box.**

> be   finish   run   talk   use   wear

1 Be quick! We .... late or we'll miss the start o the film.
2 You .... trainers when you play tennis.
3 You .... across the road. It's very dangerous
4 Shh. You .... in the library!
5 Put your phone away. You .... it in the cinen
6 I .... my homework by tomorrow.

⑤ **Complete the advice to tourists. Use must or mustn't an a verb.**

1 .... the museum. It's really interesting!
2 .... the taxis. They're very expensive. Use th metro.
3 .... a pizza restaurant. They have fantastic food.
4 .... your passport. Keep it somewhere safe!
5 .... the cathedral. It's a beautiful building

1

FIRST CONDITIONAL

We use the first conditional to talk about likely situations/
actions.

conditional clause: if + present simple	main clause/result: will + infinitive
we run,	we'll catch the bus.
we don't run,	we won't catch the bus.

The conditional clause can start or finish the sentence.
If you work hard, you'll pass your exam. (There is a comma
after the conditional clause.)
You'll pass your exam if you work hard. (There is no comma
after the main clause.)

We can use the first conditional to talk about the future, but
we use a present tense verb after *if*.
*If you **work** hard, you'll pass your exam.*
NOT If you will work hard, you'll pass your exam.)

PRACTICE

Complete the first conditional sentences with the correct
form of the verbs in brackets.

If I .... (see) my brother, I .... (tell)
him to text you.

You .... (hurt) yourself if you .... (fall)
over on the ice.

If we .... (not catch) the 10 o'clock bus, we
.... (have) to wait for an hour.

You .... (be) late for school if you ....
(not leave) soon.

If the music .... (be) loud, it ....
(wake) the baby.

2 **Put the words in order to make first conditional sentences.
Don't forget to add commas to some sentences.**

1 earn / get / a holiday job / I / I'll / if / money.

   If ....

2 a bike / buy / enough money / have / I / I'll / If

   I'll ....

3 a / bike / to go / have / I / I'll / If / use / to school / it

   If ....

4 my bike / fit / get / I / I'll / If / ride / to school

   I'll ....

5 a bike / by bus / don't have / enough money / for / go / I /
   I'll / If / money / to school

   If ....

6 by bus / fit / get / go / I / I / If / to school / won't

   I won't ....

SOMETHING, ANYTHING, NOTHING, ETC.

	people	things	places
some	someone/somebody	something	somewhere
any	anyone/anybody	anything	anywhere
every	everyone/everybody	everything	everywhere
no	no one/nobody	nothing	nowhere

- We can use *someone* or *somebody* for a person we don't know.
  *There's **someone**/**somebody** in the swimming pool.* (= I don't know who it is.)

- Use *anyone* or *anybody* in questions and negative sentences.
  *Is **anyone** coming swimming with me?*
  *I don't know **anybody** in the team.* (not ~~I don't know nobody in the team.~~)

- We can use *something* for a thing we don't know.
  *I've got **something** in my eye.* (= I don't know what it is.)

- We can also use *something* to make an offer.
  *Would you like **something** to drink?*

- Use *anything* in questions and negative sentences.
  *Are you doing **anything** at the weekend?*
  *Do you want **anything** to eat?*

- We use *no one/nobody* and *nothing* to talk about 'no people' or 'no things'. We use a positive verb with *no one/nobody* and *nothing*.
  ***No one**/**Nobody** went to school yesterday.* (= There were no people at school yesterday.)
  *We have **nothing** to do this afternoon.*
  (not ~~We don't have nothing to do this afternoon.~~)

- We use *everyone/everybody* and *everything* to talk about 'all people' and 'all things'. We use a singular verb with *everyone/everybody*, and *everything*.
  *Tom is friendly with **everyone**.*
  ***Everybody** likes Tom.* (not ~~Everyone like Tom.~~)
  ***Everything** in this shop is expensive.* (not ~~Everything in this shop are expensive.~~)

PRACTICE

3 Rewrite these sentences using the words in brackets.

1 All the people in my class enjoy football. (everyone)

....

2 There are no people here. (nobody)

....

3 That is a person I know. (someone)

....

4 My bag is empty. (nothing)

....

5 Did you phone a person this morning? (anyone)

....

6 Where are all the people? (everybody)

....

4 <u>Underline</u> and correct the mistakes in the sentences. One sentence is correct.

1 Nothing doesn't worry me.

2 Everything in the garden are beautiful.

3 Nobody didn't come to see us yesterday.

4 Somebody phoned me yesterday evening.

5 Everyone love summer holidays.

RESENT PERFECT

ositive/Negative forms

/You/We/They	have/'ve have not/haven't	been to Australia.
He/She/It	has/'s has not/hasn't	learned to cook.

estion forms and short answers

Have	I/you/we/they	been to Australia?
Has	he/she/it	
Yes,	I/you/we/they	have.
	he/she/it	has.
No,	I/you/we/they	haven't.
	he/she/it	hasn't.

he past participle form of regular verbs is the same as the ast simple:

alk – **walked**

mile – **smiled**

ou will need to learn the past participle form of irregular erbs. Here are some common examples.

be	**been**
break	**broken**
come	**came**
do	**done**
eat	**eaten**
find	**found**
get	**got**
have	**had**
meet	**met**
see	**seen**
speak	**spoken**

- We can use the present perfect to talk about our experiences:
  I've seen all the Harry Potter films, but *I haven't read* the books.

- We do not usually say when something happened with the present perfect:
  I've been to India. (not ~~I've been to India last year.~~)

- Use the past simple to say when something happened:
  I went to India *last year*.

- We often use *ever* in present perfect questions (*ever* = in your life):
  Have you ever been to India?
  Have you ever met someone famous?

- We can use *never* to talk about things we have not done in our life:
  She's never been to India.
  He's never met anyone famous.

PRACTICE

1 Complete the sentences with the present perfect of the verb in brackets.

1 My father .... (meet) the president of our country.

2 I .... (never be) in a plane.

3 .... you ever .... (travel) to another country?

4 My brother .... (win) a prize at school.

5 My sister .... (never swim) in the sea.

2 Choose the correct verbs in italics.

Ben: Hi, Tim. **(1)** I *didn't see / haven't seen* you last week. Where were you?

Tim: On holiday in the US. **(2)** *Did you ever go / Have you ever been* there?

Ben: No, I **(3)** *didn't / haven't*. But my parents **(4)** *went / have been* there three or four times.

Tim: You should go. I **(5)** *went / have been* twice.

SHOULD | SHOULDN'T

- Use *should/shouldn't* + infinitive to give someone advice:
  You **should do** more exercise.
  You **shouldn't eat** too much before you go to bed.

Positive/Negative forms

I/He/She/ You/We/ They	**should** eat more fruit and vegetables.
	shouldn't eat a lot of fast food.

Question forms and short answers

Should	I/you/we/they he/she	ask someone to help me?
Yes,	I/you/we/they he/she	**should.**
No,	I/you/we/they he/she	**shouldn't.**

3 Complete the table with this advice to students before an exam.

> Go to bed early.

> Work late the day before

> Spend too much time alone.

> Worry.

> Ask parents or friends to help you

You should ...	You shouldn't ...

4 Complete the sentences with *should/shouldn't* and verb the box.

> arrive   drink   eat   get   ride   wear

1 If it's very hot, you .... lots of water.

2 If it's cold, you .... your hat and coat.

3 You .... too much sugar. It's bad for your

4 You .... that bike. There's a problem with

5 If you're always tired, you .... more sleep

6 Students .... late for school.

3

RESENT PERFECT WITH *FOR* AND *SINCE*

can use the present perfect with *since* and *for* to talk about
nething that started in the past and continues up to the
sent.

known my best friend **for** a long time. (= I still know my
t friend now.)

the present perfect with *for* to talk about a period of time.
studied English **for six years**.
ve lived in Berlin **for three months**.

the present perfect with *since* to talk about when a
ation started.
studied English **since 2015**.
ve lived in Berlin **since June**.

CTICE

omplete the table with time phrases from the box.

> 24 hours   6 o'clock   400 years   last November
> my birthday   October 12th   ten minutes
> the end of May   three weeks
> 12 months   yesterday

	since

oose the correct words or phrases in italics.

I haven't seen my sister for *last weekend / two weeks*.

My parents have been married for *1999 / 14 years*.

I haven't done any homework since *last weekend / two weeks*.

I've had my bike since *January / six months*.

My father has worked as a doctor for *1994 / 23 years*.

Juan has played the guitar since *the age of nine / nine years*.

MAY/MIGHT

Use *may* and *might* (*not*) + infinitive when we are not sure
about something in the present or the future.
Jenny **might** be too busy to help us at the moment.
It **may be** sunny tomorrow.
My parents **might buy** a new car next week.
It **may not rain** this evening.
We **might not go** to Jack's party at the weekend.

PRACTICE

3 Ben asks six of his friends if they are coming to his party.
Here are their replies. Who is going to the party?

1 I might come. I'll tell you tomorrow. (Suzie)

2 Not sure, I may have to check with my parents. (Hannah)

3 Yes, I'll be there. (Tom)

4 Probably not. I may have to go out with my parents. (Mike)

5 Of course. What time does it start? (Julie)

6 I hope so, but I may have to work. (Ryan)

4 Match sentences 1–6 with sentences a–f.

1 I'm feeling really tired.
2 I'm really hungry.
3 I may phone my dad.
4 I might not go to school.
5 My dad has a new job.
6 Don't call me tonight.

a He might know where my books are.
b I'm not feeling very well.
c We might move house.
d I might be busy.
e I might go to bed early.
f I might have something to eat.

14

THE PASSIVE

We form the passive by using the correct form of *be* followed by the past participle.

active	passive
We feed our cat twice a day.	*Our cat is fed twice a day.*
They built our school in 2012.	*Our school was built in 2012.*

We use passive verbs rather than active verbs when:

- we don't know who did the action.
  My bike was stolen last week. (I don't know who stole it.)
- we are more interested in who or what is affected by the action of the verb than who or what does the action.
  My trainers were made in China. (The focus is on my trainers rather than where someone made them.)
  We were given a lot of homework to do in the holidays. (Here, *we* are the focus, not the homework or the teachers who gave the homework.)

- To say who did something, we use the passive + *by* + the person or thing:
  My stolen bike was found by the police.
  These shoes were made by my grandfather.

PRACTICE

1 Complete the sentences with the present simple passive form of the verbs in brackets.

1 A lot of tea .... (grow) in China.

2 Millions of bottles of water .... (sell) every d[a]

3 Interesting films .... (show) at the cinema in my town.

4 Our furniture .... (make) out of wood.

5 The road .... (close) today because of the storm.

2 Complete the sentences with the past simple passive form of the verbs in the box.

build   close   give   send   take   tell

1 Our house .... five years ago.

2 We .... how to get out if there was a fire in t[he] building.

3 The car factory in our town .... two years a[go] Nobody works there now.

4 I .... a new watch for my birthday.

5 These photos .... on my phone.

6 I .... this email yesterday.

RESENT PERFECT WITH *JUST*, *ALREADY* and *YET*

use *just*, *already* and *yet* with present perfect verbs to about things that have happened before now but have a nection with now.

Use *just* to talk about something that happened a short time go. We put *just* between *have/has* and the past participle.
've just spoken to my friend Paul.
*My dad **has just got** home from school.*

ady
se *already* to talk about something that happened before ow or before we expected.
We've already told Mike where the match is. (Mike knows, so ou don't need to tell him.)
ave you already finished your homework? That was quick! The speaker did not expect this.)
ve already had my lunch. (I'm not hungry now.)

put *already* between *have/has* and the past participle or the end of a sentence.
*e **already** seen him. / I've seen him **already**.*

(= until now) is used in negative sentences and questions alk about things we plan to do in the future, but which not done. *Yet* is placed at the end of a sentence:
ve you finished your homework **yet**?
aven't read your email **yet**.

PRACTICE

3 **Put the word in brackets in the correct position in these sentences.**

1 Have you .... tided your bedroom .... ? (yet)

2 They've .... finished .... their school project. (already)

3 I'm really hot. I've .... run home from college .... (just)

4 I don't want to watch that programme. I've .... seen it .... twice. (already)

5 Tania doesn't want .... to go to bed .... She isn't tired. (yet)

4 **Put the words in order to make sentences.**

1 I / haven't / my / new / shoes / worn / yet.

....

2 eating. / finished / just / We've

....

3 already / all / friends. / I've / my / texted

....

4 book / finished / Have / reading / that / yet? / you

....

5 brother. / I've / just / my / older / phoned

....

Phrasal verb builder

A phrasal verb is a verb with two or three parts. The meaning of the verb is sometimes different from the meaning of its separate parts. Phrasal verbs can combine verbs with prepositions or adverbs.

This section focuses on phrasal verbs related to four topics: **getting about, in the morning, people and communication** and **other phrasal verbs**.

GETTING ABOUT

1 Match the phrasal verbs to the definitions below.

> come in   get back   come round
> pick (someone) up   take off

.... = return
.... = leave the ground (a plane)
.... = visit someone's house
.... = enter a place
.... = collect someone from somewhere

PRACTICE

2 Complete the sentences with the correct form of the phrasal verbs from Exercise 1.

1 Our plane .... at three o'clock tomorrow afternoon.

2 We're away for a few days, but I'll call you when we ....

3 Yesterday evening my dad .... from school in his car.

4 You look tired. Why don't you .... and sit down.

5 I .... to your house yesterday but you were out.

3 Write a sentence using each of the phrasal verbs.

IN THE MORNING

1 Match the phrasal verbs to the definitions below.

> get up   go out   put something on
> take something off   wake up

.... = stop wearing
.... = stop sleeping
.... = get out of bed
.... = leave
.... = start wearing

PRACTICE

2 Complete the sentences with the correct form of phrasal verbs from Exercise 1.

1 I usually .... at 6.30 an then listen to music for 20 minutes.

2 My dad calls me at 6.50 and I .... out of bed.

3 Next I .... my night clc and have a shower.

4 Then I .... my school uniform .... and have breakfast.

5 I usually .... at about to catch the bus to school.

3 Write a sentence using each of the phrasal verbs

EOPLE AND COMMUNICATION

Match the phrasal verbs to the definitions below.

> call someone back   find out   get on with someone
>   grow up   look after

.... = become an adult
.... = return a phone call
.... = get information about
.... = take care of
.... = be friendly with someone

CTICE

omplete the sentences with the correct form of the hrasal verbs from the box.

I need to .... my little sister while my parents are out.

I .... very well with all my brothers and sisters.

There's a car outside our house. I want to .... who it belongs to.

Sorry, I have to hurry. I'll .... you .... tomorrow.

We live in the city now, but my parents .... in a small village.

rite a sentence using each of the phrasal verbs.

OTHER PHRASAL VERBS

1 Match the phrasal verbs to the definitions below.

> fill in   give back   lie down   try on   turn off

.... = usually something you do before you go to sleep
.... = stop a machine or light from working
.... = write information on a form
.... = give something to the person who gave it to you
.... = put on clothes to see if they fit

PRACTICE

2 Complete the sentences with the correct form of the phrasal verbs from Exercise 1.

1 I've got a bad headache, so I'm going to ....

2 Don't forget to .... the lights when you leave the building.

3 I always .... shoes .... before I buy them.

4 To get a passport you have to .... a lot of forms.

5 When are you going to .... the book I lent you?

3 Write a sentence using each of the phrasal verbs.

Irregular verbs

verb	past simple	past participle
be	was / were	was / were
become	became	become
begin	began	begun
break	broke	broken
build	built	built
burn	burnt / burned	burnt / burned
buy	bought	bought
catch	caught	caught
choose	chose	chosen
come	came	come
cost	cost	cost
cut	cut	cut
do	did	done
draw	drew	drawn
dream	dreamt / dreamed	dreamt / dreamed
drink	drank	drunk
drive	drove	driven
eat	ate	eaten
fall	fell	fallen
feel	felt	felt
find	found	found
fly	flew	flown
forget	forgot	forgotten
get	got	got / gotten
give	gave	given
go	went	been / gone
grow	grew	grown
have	had	had
hear	heard	heard
hit	hit	hit
hurt	hurt	hurt
keep	kept	kept
know	knew	known
learn	learnt / learned	learnt / learned
leave	left	left
let	let	let
lie	lied	lied
lose	lost	lost
make	made	made
mean	meant	meant
meet	met	met
pay	paid	paid
put	put	put
read	read	read
ride	rode	ridden
run	ran	run
say	said	said
see	saw	seen
sell	sold	sold

verb	past simple	past participle
send	sent	sent
show	showed	shown
shut	shut	shut
sing	sang	sung
sit	sat	sat
sleep	slept	slept
speak	spoke	spoken
spell	spelt / spelled	spelt / spelled
spend	spent	spent
stand	stood	stood
steal	stole	stolen
swim	swam	swum
take	took	taken
teach	taught	taught
tell	told	told
think	thought	thought
throw	threw	thrown
understand	understood	understood
wake	woke	woken
wear	wore	worn
win	won	won
write	wrote	written

OW TO MAKE YOUR WRITING BETTER: DJECTIVES

make a sentence more interesting, we can use adjectives.

ook at the pairs of sentences. Underline the adjectives in each b sentence.

a There was a chair in the corner of the room.
b There was a <u>comfortable</u> chair in the corner of the room.

a We had lunch in a restaurant.
b We had lunch in a small, friendly restaurant.

a A woman showed me the way home.
b A kind woman showed me the way home.

a I knew I had made a mistake.
b I knew I had made a big mistake.

ook at Exercise 1 again. Decide if the sentences are true r false.

djectives …

describe people or things.

usually come after the person or thing they describe.

can make sentences more interesting because they add more information.

omplete the sentences with an adjective from the box.

| expensive | heavy | important | lovely | modern |

He was carrying a .... suitcase.

I have an .... message for you.

She lives in a .... apartment.

We had a .... day in the park.

She was wearing an .... jacket.

4 We often use adjectives to talk about good or nice things. Choose the two adjectives which can replace good or nice in each sentence.

1 It was a very good film. (*exciting / friendly / funny*)

2 She was wearing a nice dress. (*beautiful / lovely / clever*)

3 That's a good idea. (*brilliant / famous / great*)

4 A nice doctor helped me. (*friendly / favourite / kind*)

5 The weather was nice. (*sunny / clever / pleasant*)

6 We had some good food. (*great / hungry / excellent*)

5 We often use adjectives to talk about very good or very bad things. <u>Underline</u> the adjectives which mean 'very good' or 'very bad' in each sentence. Then add them to the table.

1 It was a nice day. We had a <u>wonderful</u> meal.

2 We didn't play tennis because the weather was terrible.

3 I loved the film. It was amazing!

4 I didn't like the food. It was horrible.

5 We watched a film, but it was awful!

6 I think she's a fantastic singer. I love her songs.

very good	very bad
wonderful	

HOW TO MAKE YOUR WRITING BETTER: ADVERBS AND INTERESTING VERBS

1 Look at the pairs of sentences. <u>Underline</u> the adverbs in each b sentence.

1 a I ran home.
b I <u>quickly</u> ran home.

2 a The children were playing in the garden.
b The children were playing happily in the garden.

3 a I read the invitation.
b I read the invitation carefully.

4 a She opened the letter.
b She opened the letter slowly.

5 a I couldn't see because it was cloudy.
b I couldn't see well because it was cloudy.

2 Look at Exercise 1 again. Decide if the sentences are true or false.

1 Adverbs can describe how someone does something.

2 Most adverbs end in *-ly*.

3 Adverbs always come before the verb.

4 Adverbs can make sentences more interesting, because they describe actions.

3 Choose the best adverb in each sentence.

1 A man called my name *loudly / terribly*.

2 The children ate their pizzas *kindly / hungrily*.

3 He spoke *clearly / cheaply*.

4 My mum was driving very *noisily / fast*.

5 She *carefully / busily* picked up the young bird.

6 We found the boat *easily / loudly*.

7 Everyone in the team played *quickly / well*, and we won the game!

8 She sang the song *beautifully / highly*.

4 Complete the sentences with the adverb in brackets. Choose the correct place to put the adverb.

1 The .... police officer spoke to me .... (angrily)
The police officer spoke to me angrily.

2 I .... read the .... letter. (quickly)

3 She closed .... the door ....(quiet

4 He .... carried the hot drinks into the .... sitting room. (carefully)

5 We walked .... through ....the pa (slowly)

6 Mark didn't .... sleep .... last nigh (well)

5 Sometimes we can use a more interesting verb instead of a verb and an adverb. <u>Underline</u> the verb in each b sentence which matches the verb + adverb in the first sentence.

1 a I <u>went</u> to the bus stop <u>quickly</u>.
b I hurried to the bus stop.

2 a Everyone was <u>speaking loudly</u> at the same time.
b Everyone was shouting at the same time.

3 a <u>They</u> were <u>sitting quietly</u> in the garden.
b They were relaxing in the garden.

4 a We <u>got into</u> the water <u>quickly</u>.
b We jumped into the water.

5 a I <u>put</u> the letter <u>quickly</u> into the bin.
b I threw the letter into the bin.

6 a 'I'm lost,' she <u>said sadly</u>.
b 'I'm lost,' she cried.

6 Complete the sentences with the verbs in the box.

| jumped | ran | relaxed | shouted | threw |

1 She .... into the room and picked up the ph

2 'Go away!' he ....

3 We sat down and .... for a few minutes.

4 The girl .... onto her bike and rode away.

5 He .... the map onto the fire.

Read the email. Underline six mistakes with verb forms.

Hi Jo,

I go swimming next Saturday. My cousin are here at the moment, and he love swimming. Are you want to come too? There's a swimming pool on Wood Road. We can to get the bus. I meet you at the bus stop.

Sam

Write the email from Exercise 1 correctly.

....

....

....

....

This email has more information. Read it and choose the correct verbs in italics.

Hi Jo,

I **(1)** *goes / 'm going / want go* swimming next Saturday. My cousin **(2)** *is / was / am* here at the moment and he **(3)** *is love / loves / loving* swimming. **(4)** *You want / Does you want / Do you want* to come too? There's a swimming pool on Wood Road. I **(5)** *never been / 've never been / never went* there, but Max **(6)** *went / has been / been* yesterday and he says it's great. We can **(7)** *get / getting / gets* the bus. I **(8)** *'m meeting / can to meet / can meet* you at the bus stop.

Look at Exercise 3 again. Find an example of these things.

the present continuous for future plans ....

the past simple for an action in the past ....

the present perfect for an experience at some time in the past ....

a modal verb ....

Complete the email below with the correct form of the verbs in brackets.

Hi Sara,

I **(1)** .... (go) to a concert in Manchester next Saturday. My uncle **(2)** .... (buy) me two tickets for my birthday last month. The concert **(3)** .... (start) at eight o'clock. My friend Sam wants **(4)** .... (come) too. I think you **(5)** .... (meet) him a few times. We can **(6)** .... (go) for a pizza first if you want.

6 Use these notes to write an email. Try to use different verb forms correctly.

- ask a friend to come to a water park with you next Saturday

- say where it is

- say how you can get there

USE LINKING WORDS AND RELATIVE PRONOUNS TO MAKE LONGER SENTENCES

1 Read the story. How many sentences are there?

> Dan woke up. He got out of bed. He didn't look at his clock. He opened the fridge. It was almost empty. He was hungry. He decided to go out for some food. He went to a café. It was closed. It was only 6.30 in the morning!

2 Read the same story. This time, the sentences are linked with linking words. Underline the linking words.

> Dan woke up <u>and</u> got out of bed. He didn't look at his clock. He opened the fridge, but it was almost empty. He was hungry, so he decided to go out for some food. He went to a café, but it was closed because it was only 6.30 in the morning!

3 Choose the correct linking words in italics.

1 I wanted to go to the cinema, *but* / *so* I didn't have any money.

2 It was late *and* / *because* I was very tired.

3 It was cold, *but* / *so* I put on my coat.

4 We couldn't play tennis *but* / *because* it was raining.

5 I invited Sam, *because* / *but* he didn't want to come.

6 It was sunny, *but* / *so* we decided to have a barbecue.

4 Look at the a and b sentences. Underline the linking words that join the sentences in b.

1 **a** He showed me a photo. It wasn't very clear.
   b He showed me a photo which wasn't very clear.

2 **a** I saw a girl. She looked scared.
   b I saw a girl who looked scared.

3 **a** I saw a man in the street. He was singing.
   b I saw a man in the street who was singing.

4 **a** The man was carrying a bag. It looked heavy.
   b The man was carrying a bag that looked heavy.

5 Look at Exercise 4 again. Choose the correct words in italics.

1 We can use *who* / *which* and *that* to write about people.

2 We can use *who* / *which* and *that* to write about things.

6 Choose the correct words in italics to complete the stori

> Emma was on holiday with her family in a new city, and they wanted to go to a museum. They were lost. Then they saw a girl **(1)** *which* / *who* was holding a map. The girl showed Emma her map. But she gave Emma some directions **(2)** *which* / *who* were wrong! Emma and her family found the museum, but it was closed when they arrived!

> Martin was in the city centre with his mum. He wanted to buy some new shoes, so he went to a shoe shop. He saw some black shoes **(3)** *which* / *who* he liked. They were very expensive. His mum didn't have much money. She spoke to an assistant **(4)** *which* / *who* worked in the shop. The assistant showed Martin some cheaper shoes. Martin liked these ones, too, so he bought them.

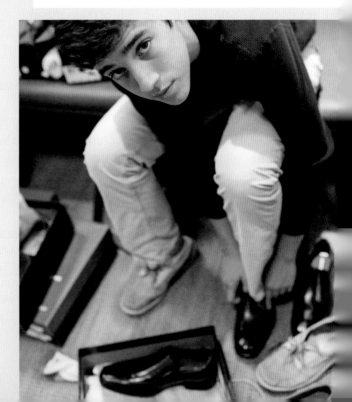

WRITING PART 6: A SHORT MESSAGE

Read the exam task. How many things must you write about in your email? How many words should you write?

You want to borrow a bike from your English friend, Mike. Write an email to Mike.

In your email:

- **ask** Mike if **you can borrow** his bike
- explain **why** you need it
- say when you will **give it back**

Write 25 words or more.

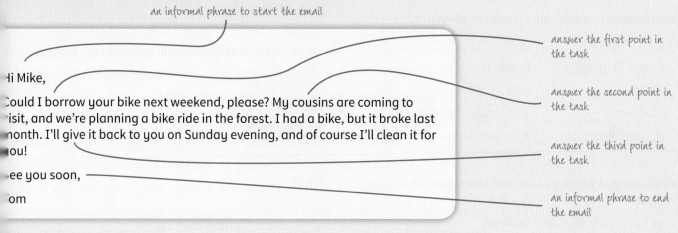

an informal phrase to start the email

answer the first point in the task

answer the second point in the task

answer the third point in the task

an informal phrase to end the email

Hi Mike,

Could I borrow your bike next weekend, please? My cousins are coming to visit, and we're planning a bike ride in the forest. I had a bike, but it broke last month. I'll give it back to you on Sunday evening, and of course I'll clean it for you!

See you soon,

Tom

MODEL ANSWER

KEY LANGUAGE AND IDEAS FOR EMAILS

Opening an email:
Hi Tom,   Hello

Closing an email:
Love,   See you soon,   Bye,   Thanks ...

Inviting someone:
Would you like to ...?   Do you want to ...?

Making a suggestion:
Why don't you/we ...?   You/We could ...   Let's ...
How about ...?   What about ...?

Making an offer or promise:
I could ... if you like.   I can ... if you want.   I'll ...

Making a request:
Could I/you ...?   Can I/you ...?   Is it OK if I ...?

Giving good news:
Can you believe it?   Great news!   Guess what?

Giving bad news:
I'm sorry, but ...   I'm afraid ...

Linking words and phrases:
and   but   so   because

Informal language:
Contractions: *I'm   you're   she's*
Informal words and phrases: *amazing   brilliant   OK*

2 Complete the suggestions with the words in the box.

> could   don't   Let's   Shall   Why

1 Why .... we get the bus together?

2 We .... meet outside the cinema.

3 .... we buy the tickets online?

4 .... get the train.

5 .... don't we go for a pizza after the show?

3 Match sentence beginnings 1–5 with endings a–e.

1 Could I borrow   a with my homework?

2 Can you help me   b laptop?

3 Is it OK   c your bike?

4 Could I stay   d if I bring my friend Jack?

5 Can you bring your   e at your house on Saturday night?

4 Write sentences about good or bad news. Use the word in brackets.

1 I've passed all my exams. (believe)

Can you believe it? I've passed all my exams!

2 I can't come to your party. (afraid)

....

3 I'll be a bit late. (sorry)

....

4 I won the competition! (guess)

....

5 Read the email. Underline five verbs where you can use contractions.

Hi Joe,

My cousin Beth is coming to visit on Saturday, and I am really excited. She is very good at computer games. I have got a new game and we are going to play some games together. Do you want to come too? I will call you later.

Sam

6 Read the exam task. What information should you include in your email?

Your English friend Laura has invited you to go to a concert with her on Saturday, but you can't go. Write an email to Laura.

In your email:
- **say** that you **can't go** on Saturday
- explain **why** you can't go
- suggest **another day** to meet.

Write **25 words** or more.

7 Before you write your email, complete the table with ideas.

You can't go on Saturday	*I'm sorry, but …*
Why?	*… because …*
Another day to meet	*Why don't we …?*

8 Write your email, using your notes from Exercise 7.

9 Check your email and make changes if necessary.

☐ Have you answered all the points in Laura's email?

☐ Have you used a suitable phrase to open and close your email?

☐ Have you used a range of language?

☐ Have you used linking words to make longer senten

☐ Have you used contractions and informal language

☐ Have you counted your words?

WRITING PART 7: A STORY

ad the exam task. How many words should you write?

ok at the three pictures.

te the story shown in the pictures.

te **35 words** or more.

DEL ANSWER

ark got up and looked outside. He
as happy because it was a sunny
y. He decided to play football.
then found his football and
rried outside. Next, he called his
ends. Later, his friends arrived, and
ey played together. They had a
onderful time!

— this tells the first part of the story

— past simple verbs for the main events in the story

— adjectives and adverbs make the story more interesting

— this tells the second part of the story

— this tells the third part of the story

LANGUAGE AND IDEAS FOR STORIES

e the story an interesting title:
robbery   A day out

past simple and past continuous verbs:
k got up   It was raining

time expressions:
t   then   later   the next day

adjectives to describe people, places and feelings:
ndly   kind   busy   excited   angry

adverbs:
kly   slowly   carefully

interesting verbs:
ied   ran   shouted

2 Complete the story with the past simple or past continuous form of the verbs in brackets.

A surprise visit

Mary was at home one afternoon. She **(1)** .... (feel) bored because it **(2)** .... (rain). Suddenly, Mary's friend Sara **(3)** .... (arrive) at the house. She **(4)** .... (carry) a pizza in a box, and a video game. Mary was very happy! Mary and Sara **(5)** .... (eat) the pizza together and **(6)** .... (play) the game.

3 Choose the correct time expressions in *italics* to complete the stories.

Max decided to make a cake. **(1)** *First / Next*, he went to the supermarket to buy some eggs and butter. **(2)** *Suddenly / Next* he mixed everything together quickly and put the cake in the oven. **(3)** *Finally / First*, the cake was ready! Max ate a big slice, and it was fantastic!

Paula was cycling home. **(4)** *First / Suddenly*, she saw a puppy in the road. It was on its own, and it looked sad. It was her friend Sam's dog. Paula called the dog to her. **(5)** *Then / Finally*, she phoned Sam. **(6)** *Finally / Next*, Sam arrived. He was very pleased, and the dog was so excited!

4 Cross out the adjective that is not possible in each sentence.

1 I was feeling angry / happy / tired / tall.
2 The waiter was very polite / empty / kind / friendly.
3 The town was quite busy / quiet / pleased / old.
4 She was wearing a blue / big / quick / pretty hat.
5 It was a boring / great / high / brilliant film.
6 He was carrying a small / black / ready / new suitcase.

5 Read the exam task. Before you write your story, make notes on your ideas in the table.

Look at the pictures.

Write the story shown in the pictures.
Write **35 words** or more.

Picture 1	
Picture 2	
Picture 3	

6 Write your story, using your notes from Exercise 5.

7 Check your story and make changes if necessary.

☐ Have you written about all three pictures?

☐ Have you used past simple verbs?

☐ Have you used adjectives and adverbs to make you story interesting?

☐ Have you counted your words?

GIVING PERSONAL INFORMATION

Listen to two students giving personal information. Complete the table.

	Pablo	Lucia
Age		
From		

KEY LANGUAGE AND IDEAS FOR GIVING PERSONAL INFORMATION

Saying your name:
My name is / My name's ...

Saying your age:
I'm ... years old.

Saying where you come from:
I come from ...

Saying where you live:
I live in ...

Match the sentence beginnings 1–4 with endings a–d. Listen again and check.

1 My
2 I come
3 I'm fourteen
4 I live

a in Milan.
b name's Pablo.
c from Madrid.
d years old.

TALKING ABOUT HABITS, LIKES AND DISLIKES

1 Listen to Sophie talking about her habits. Which activities does she talk about?

> doing homework   going to the cinema
> meeting friends   playing football   playing tennis
> watching TV

KEY LANGUAGE AND IDEAS FOR TALKING ABOUT HABITS

I sometimes ...
I often ...
I usually ...
I always ...
I never ...
I ... every day/every weekend/on Saturdays.

Use words like *sometimes*, *often*, etc. with the present simple form of verbs:
*I **sometimes meet** my friends.*
*I **often** go to the cinema.*
*I **go out** with friends **every weekend**.*

Notice that *sometimes, often, usually*, etc. come before the main verb, but after the verb *be*. Phrases such as *every day, every weekend, on Saturdays* come at the end:
*I **never play** football.*
*I'm **never** late.*
*I **often play** video games.*
*I **play** video games **every day**.*

2 Choose the correct options in *italics*. Listen again and check.

1 I *always get up / get up always* early.
2 I *never am / am never* late for school.
3 I *usually do / do usually* my homework when I get home from school.
4 I don't *often watch / watch often* TV.
5 I usually play tennis *in Saturdays / on Saturdays*.
6 I *meet sometimes / sometimes meet* my friends at the weekend.

3 Listen to Sam talking about his likes and dislikes. What's his favourite sport?

KEY LANGUAGE AND IDEAS FOR TALKING ABOUT LIKES AND DISLIKES

I like …
I don't like …
I love …
I prefer …
I enjoy …
My favourite (sport, food, etc.) *is …*

Use *like*, *love* and *prefer* with a noun, an *-ing* form of a verb, or an infinitive.
*I **like/love/prefer adventure films**.*
*I **like/love/prefer going shopping**.*
*I **like/love/prefer to go** out with friends.*

Use *enjoy* with a noun or an *-ing* form of a verb.
*I **enjoy basketball**.*
*I **enjoy going** on holiday.*
~~I enjoy to go shopping~~.

Say *I prefer … to …* .
*I **prefer** basketball **to** tennis.*

4 Complete the sentences with the words in the box. Listen again and check.

> don't   favourite   like   listening   prefer

1 I .... maths and science.
2 I .... like art.
3 I enjoy .... to music.
4 I .... football to tennis.
5 Basketball is my .... sport.

GIVING OPINIONS AND REASONS

1 Listen to a conversation about different activities. Which activity do both people like?

2 Complete the conversation with words from the box. Listen again and check.

> about   do   do   don't   fun   going   love
> prefer   think   what

Girl: **(1)** .... you like swimming?
Boy: Yes, I **(2)** .... It's fun. What **(3)** .... you?
Girl: No, I **(4)** .... like swimming. I **(5)** .... it's boring. But I love **(6)** .... to the cinema. It's really interesting. **(7)** .... do you think?
Boy: No, I think going to the cinema is expensive. I **(8)** .... to watch films at home. My favourite activity is cycling. Do you think cycling is **(9)** .... ?
Girl: Yes, I do. I **(10)** .... cycling!

3 We often give reasons to explain our opinions. Listen to three people giving reasons for their opinions. Choose the reason that each person gives.

1 I like travelling because
   a you meet interesting people.
   b you learn about different countries.
2 I don't like skateboarding because
   a it's dangerous.
   b it's boring.
3 I love this computer game because
   a it's exciting.
   b I'm very good at it.

KEY LANGUAGE AND IDEAS FOR GIVING OPINIONS AND REASONS

Asking for opinions:
Do you like …?
Do you think … is/are (fun/interesting/exciting …)?
Do you prefer … or …?
What about you?
What do you think?

Giving opinions:
I think … is/are (boring/difficult …)
I don't think … is/are (dangerous/expensive …)
For me, … is (fun/interesting …)

Giving reasons:
I like … because …
I think … is interesting because …

Use *is* with singular nouns and *are* with plural nouns
*Do you think camping **is** fun?*
*I think video games **are** fun.*

Use *I don't think* + a positive verb:
*I **don't think** reading **is** interesting.* NOT *~~I think it isn't very interesting~~.*
*I **don't think** football is fun.* NOT *~~I think football isn't f~~*

4 Complete the sentences with your own opinions o reasons. Listen and compare your ideas.

1 I *like / don't like* reading because …
2 I *love / hate* football because …
3 I *like / don't like* shopping because …

DEALING WITH PROBLEMS

1 Listen to three conversations. Complete the sentences with the words you hear.

1 .... that please?

2 .... the question, please?

3 Could you .... , please?

2 Find and <u>underline</u> the mistake in each question. Listen again and check.

1 Could you repeat again that, please?

2 Can you repeat me the question, please?

3 Could you say again, please?

3 Listen to two people talking. What are they trying to describe?

Item 1	**a** a piece of clothing
Item 2	**b** a kind of food
Item 3	**c** a game

KEY LANGUAGE AND IDEAS FOR DEALING WITH PROBLEMS

Asking someone to repeat:
Can/Could you repeat that, please?
Can/Could you repeat the question, please?
Can/Could you say that again, please?

When you don't know the word for something:
I'm not sure what the word is, but it's ... (a sport, a kind of food)
It's something you use when you ... (play football, cook)
I don't know the word, but it's something you ... (wear, eat)
I'm not sure what this is called, but it's a kind of ... (animal, plant, game).

4 Complete what the people say with one word in each gap. Listen again and check.

1 I'm .... sure what the .... is, but you often play this on the beach.

2 I'm not sure .... this is .... , but it's something you wear around your neck.

3 I don't .... what the word .... , but it's something you eat.

AGREEING AND DISAGREEING

1 Listen to a conversation about playing a musical instrument. What do the people agree about?

1 It's important to practise.

2 It's very difficult.

3 Lessons are always very expensive.

KEY LANGUAGE AND IDEAS FOR AGREEING AND DISAGREEING

Agreeing:
Yes, I agree with you.
I agree with you that ...
Exactly!
That's true.

Disagreeing:
I'm not sure about that. I think ...
I don't know. I think ...
Yes, but ...

2 Complete part of the conversation with the phrases in the box. Listen again and check.

> agree with you   not sure about   that's true
> yes, but

A: I think it's very difficult to learn an instrument.

B: I'm **(1)** .... that. The guitar isn't very difficult, but it's important to practise every day.

A: **(2)** .... I **(3)** .... that it's important to practise so that you can get better. I think that lessons are very expensive, too.

B: **(4)** .... you can watch lessons online and teach yourself.

1 Listen to Ana answering three questions. Does she use full sentences in her answers?

2 Listen again. Notice how she adds extra information.
1 What do you do at weekends?
2 Who do you like spending your weekends with?
3 Where do you like going shopping?
4 What do you like buying?

3 Complete Ana's answers with *or* or *because*. Listen again and check.
1 I often go shopping, ... I sometimes go to the cinema.
2 I like going shopping in London .... there are lots of good shops.
3 I like buying clothes and shoes .... I'm interested in fashion.

4 Lead Ana's answer to a longer question. Choose the correct verbs in *italics*. Listen and check.

Examiner: Now, please tell me something about presents that you buy for other people.

Ana: Well, I **(1)** *love / loved* buying presents for people. I usually **(2)** *buy / am buying* presents for people when it's their birthday. For example, last month I **(3)** *buy / bought* a T-shirt for my brother and he really **(4)** *like / liked* it. It's my friend's birthday next week, and I **(5)** *take / 'm going to take* her to the cinema as a present.

5 Choose the best answers to the questions.
1 Where do you usually meet your friends?
   a I usually meet my friends at the weekend.
   b I often meet them at the cinema, or we go for a meal together.
2 Who do you live with?
   a I share a flat with three friends.
   b I live in a small apartment in the city centre.
3 What sports can you do in your area?
   a I play tennis once a week, but I can't play very well.
   b You can play tennis and football at the sports centre near my house.
4 What time do you usually have lunch?
   a I usually have lunch at about one o'clock.
   b I usually have a sandwich and some fruit.
5 What did you eat for breakfast this morning?
   a I don't usually have breakfast, but sometimes I have some cereal.
   b I had some eggs and some orange juice.
6 How many rooms are there in your house or flat?
   a I like my bedroom because it's quite big, and you can see the park from my window.
   b There are two bedrooms, a kitchen, a living room and a bathroom, so five rooms.

6 Choose the correct verbs in *italics*. Then decide if each sentence is about the present, past or future.

I *go / went* shopping last weekend. *past*
1 I usually *have / had* dinner with my family.
2 I *meet / 'm going* to meet my friends tomorrow, because it's the weekend.
3 I sometimes *watch / 'm going to watch* films on my laptop because I love watching films.
4 I *cook / cooked* a meal for some friends last night, and it was very good.
5 I *play / 'm going to play* tennis next weekend with my friends.
6 I *buy / bought* some new shoes yesterday and some new jeans too.

7 Match one piece of extra information (a–e) with each question and answer (1–5). Listen and check.
1 A: Tell me something about what you like doing at home.
   B: I like watching films, and I enjoy playing video games.
2 A: Tell me something about what you like to eat with friends.
   B: I sometimes go to restaurants with my friends, and I prefer Italian food.
3 A: Tell me something about the clothes like to buy.
   B: My favourite thing to buy is jeans, because I like wearing them.
4 A: Tell me something about the places like to visit.
   B: I like visiting places that are near the sea.
5 A: Tell me something about the sports like to do.
   B: I like playing football. I play for a team and we have a game every Saturday.

a My team doesn't often win.
b I love swimming when the weather's hot.
c I've just got a new game.
d We went to a pizza restaurant last weekend.
e I bought some really nice jeans last week.

Practise answering the questions.

What's your name?

How old are you?

What do you usually do at weekend?

Who do you like going shopping with?

Where do you usually meet your friends?

What did you eat for breakfast this morning?

Tell me something about the clothes you like to buy.

Tell me something about the sports you like to do.

PEAKING PART 2

isten to two students doing the task. Do they talk about all the pictures?

Do you like these different hobbies? Say why or why not.

ten to one of the students answering a follow-up question. Does she give reasons for her answers?

3 Complete the sentences with the words in the box. Listen and check.

> about   agree   do   like   sure   think

A: I think video games are exciting. What do you
(1) .... ?

B: I'm not **(2)** .... about that.

A: What about taking photos? Do you **(3)** ....
taking photos?

B: I often take photos when I'm with my friends.

A: I take photos on my phone. What **(4)** .... you?

B: I like taking photos, too. I've got a camera.

A: I always go cycling at weekends. What **(5)** ....
you think about it?

B: I **(6)** .... with you that it's fun.

4 Match the opinions (1–5) with the reasons (a–e).

1 I prefer to go on holiday with friends because
2 I prefer to play team sports because
3 I don't like doing outdoor activities when the weather's bad
4 I prefer to watch films at home because
5 I prefer staying in hotels to camping because

a exercising on your own is boring.
b you can have food while you watch.
c it's more comfortable, and you don't get cold at night.
d you can have more fun with people of the same age.
e because nothing is fun when it's raining.

5 Work in pairs. Look at the pictures and complete the task. Then listen and compare your ideas. Did you discuss the same things?

Do you like these different summer activities?

6 Practise answering the follow-up questions. Then listen and compare your ideas.

- Which of these activities do you like the best?
- Do you prefer to go on holiday to the beach or the countryside?
- Do you prefer swimming in the sea or in a swimming pool?

nit 2

resent continuous

dent A

it 6

nool subjects

Mount Everest
It's 8,848 metres high.

the elephant

worse

nine

5 a melon

6 salt

7 November 11, 1918

8 Paris

9 the guitar

Unit 8

Starting off

How did you score?

First, add up your scores.

A = 0, B = 1, C = 2

Results

12 + You love the internet and social media. Maybe you should spend time doing other things as well.

8–11 You spend a lot of time online. Be careful – don't forget to do other things!

4–7 You are sometimes online, but not much. You know it can be useful, but you also like finding information in books.

0–3 Being online can be fun! Maybe you should try it more!

Extra resources

Present continuous

Student B

Unit 10

Places

1 Russia. Lake Baikal's deepest part is over 1,600 metres deep.

2 Bangladesh. It's called Cox's Bazar and is 125 km long.

3 Mont Blanc. It's 4,808 metres high.

4 Indonesia. Over 17,000 islands.

5 The Amazon. It's bigger than western Europe.

6 The Mojave Desert in North America. The temperature once got to 56.7 °C.

Unit 14

The passive

1 20

2 3,200

3 1971

4 Papua New Guinea

5 because (*beautiful* is second, *tomorrow* is third)

6 checking the time

Acknowledgements

The author would like to thank Alison Bewsher, Helen Kuffel and Andrew Reid personally for all their input.

The authors and publishers would like to thank the following contributors:

Grammar reference: Simon Haines
Writing and Speaking bank: Sheila Dignen

The authors and publishers are grateful to the following for reviewing the material during the writing process:

Spain: Kerry Davis, Anahí Eguía García, Karolina Majerova; Italy: Ellen Darling; Portugal: Diana England; Russia: Liubov Desiatova.

The authors and publishers acknowledge the following sources of copyright material and are grateful for the permissions granted. While every effort has been made, it has not always been possible to identify the sources of all the material used, or to trace all copyright holders. If any omissions are brought to our notice, we will be happy to include the appropriate acknowledgements on reprinting and in the next update to the digital edition, as applicable.

Key: U = Unit, GR = Grammar Reference, PVB = Phrasal verb builder, WB = Writing bank, SB = Speaking bank

Text

12: The Zapp family for the text and listening material adapted from the website www.argentinaalsaska.com. Reprinted with permission.

Photography

The following images are sourced from Getty Images.

1: Celia Peterson/Arabian Eye; Image Source; Ariel Skelly/Digital Vision; Jonner Images; Photo Alto/Jerome Groin/Photo Alto Agency RF Collections; SD Productions/Digital Vision; Ron Levine/Digital Vision; Compassionate Eye Foundation/DigitalVision; Simon Watson/The Image Bank; Kevin Dodge/Blend Images; R.Tsubin/Moment; **U2**: David Borland/Lonely Planet Images; Bulgac/iStock/Getty Images Plus; Photography by Abhey Singh/Moment; Spaces Images/Blend Images; Ray Kachatorian/Photodisc; Hero Images; Ben Pipe Photography/Cultura; Fuse/Corbis; monkeybusinessimages/iStock/Getty Images Plus; Tim Macpherson/Cultura; DGLimages/iStock/Getty Images Plus; Alys Tomlinson/Cultura; apomares/E+; xalanx/iStock/Getty Images Plus; sakkmesterkesakkmesterke/iStock/Getty Images Plus; Odilon Dimier/PhotoAlto Agency RF Collections; **U3**: fcafotodigital/iStock/Getty Images Plus; ushlama/iStock/Getty Images Plus; Joff Lee/Photolibrary; Westend61; Thanapa Nachiangmai/EyeEm; George Coppock/Photolibrary; baibaz/iStock/Getty Images Plus; Andrew Pini/Photolibrary; Creative Crop/DigitalVision; ClaudioVentrella/iStock/Getty Images Plus; Cipariss/iStock/Getty Images Plus; Kutay Tanir/Photodisc; Dorling Kindersley; Floortje/E+; MarkGillow/E+; Malorny/Moment; Westend61; Torie Jayne/Moment; cristianl/E+; kcline/E+; **U4**: Westend61; Rayman/Photodisc; Imgorthand/E+; Victor VIRGILE/Gamma-Rapho; Nick David/Taxi; Steve Debenport/E+; YesKatja/iStock/Getty Images Plus; susandaniels/E+; Alexander Feig/StockFood Creative; Dark Horse/Cultura; Jan-Stefan Knick/EyeEm; Rune Hellestad/Corbis Entertainment; Nicholas Eveleigh/Photodisc; fotofermer/iStock/Getty Images Plus; Science Photo Library/Getty Images Plus; malerapaso/E+; maksime/iStock/Getty Images Plus; Chuanchai Pundej/EyeEm; Richard Sharrocks/Moment; **U5**: Visual China Group; Stanley Chou - FIFA; erwai/iStock/Getty Images Plus; FatCamera/E+; Jupiterimages/Stockbyte; PeopleImages/E+; Richard Newstead/Moment; Alexander Hassenstein/Getty Images Sport; Bryn Lennon/Getty Images Sport; Maury Phillips/WireImage; Robbie Jay Barratt - AMA/Getty Images Sport; Scott Barbour/Getty Images Sport; Wavebreakmedia/iStock/Getty Images Plus; ViewStock; **U6**: Steve Debenport/iStock/Getty Images Plus; Andrew Luyten/Moment; Luis Diaz Devesa/Moment; Mark Langridge/OJO Images; Image Source/DigitalVision; tepic; © Hiya Images/Corbis; Zave Smith/Corbis; Martin Poole/The Image Bank; kenzaza/iStock/Getty Images Plus; Robert Daly/OJO Images; Westend61; Steve Prezant/Image Source; Ron Levine/DigitalVision; Steve Debenport/E+; PeopleImages/iStock/Getty Images Plus; Jeff Spicer/Stringer/Getty Images Entertainment; Paul Archuleta/Getty Images Entertainment; Marc Espolet Copyright/Moment; dlerick/E+; Classen Rafael/EyeEm; **U7**: Sir Francis Canker Photography/Moment; fotoVoyager/E+; Westend61; RainervonBrandis/iStock/Getty Images Plus; sunstock/iStock/Getty Images Plus; Brad Wilson/The Image Bank; Westend61; Richard Cummins/Lonely Planet Images; Mike Dow Photography/Moment; View Pictures/Universal Images Group; Robin Smith/Photolibrary; Anton Petrus/Moment; John Harper/Photolibrary; Josie Elias/Photolibrary; John Lamb/Photographer's Choice; **U8**: JGI/Jamie Grill/Blend Images; Katie Cawood/Moment; Paul Bradbury/OJO Images; JasonDoiy/E+; cglade/E+; Rainer Holz/Corbis; Tim Macpherson/Cultura; Steven Gottlieb/Corbis Historical; Carlo A/Moment; Jutta Klee/Corbis; fizkes/iStock/Getty Images Plus; Jeremy Maude/DigitalVision; Brianna Massey/Corbis Documentary; Henrik Sorensen/Iconica; Jacob Ammentorp Lund/iStock/Getty Images Plus; Creative Crop/DigitalVision; deepblue4you/E+; Tim Grist/EyeEm; Suparat Malipoom/EyeEm; Creative Crop/

Acknowledgements

Photodisc; Image Source; **U9**: Wladimir Bulgar/Science Photo Library; Dorling Kindersley; Julie Lemberger/Corbis Documentary; Hill Street Studios/Blend Images; Arthur Baensch/Corbis/Getty Images Plus; Hero Images; Magnilion/DigitalVision Vectors; **U10**: Education Images/Universal Images Group; Georgijevic/E+; Shobeir Ansari/Moment; Frank Carter/Lonely Planet Images; Peter Cade/The Image Bank; Stephen Shepherd/Photolibrary; Jordan Siemens/Iconica; avdeev007/E+; R9_RoNaLdO/E+; AlexSava/iStock/Getty Images Plus; Jones/Shimlock-Secret Sea Visions/Oxford Scientific; gustavofrazao/iStock/Getty Images Plus; coleong/iStock/Getty Images Plus; Missen/RooM; Martin Diebel; Riou/DigitalVision; Albrecht WeiÃer; rrocio/E+; Philip Lee Harvey/Cultura; **U11**: Tetra Images; Halfpoint/iStock/Getty Images Plus; SuHP/Image Source; Mike Kemp/Blend Images; Bulgac/iStock/Getty Images Plus; Kolostock/Blend Images; gbh007/iStock/Getty Images Plus; Chris Bennett/Aurora; adventtr/E+; PeopleImages/E+; U12: 1001Love/iStock/Getty Images Plus; Darran Rees/Darran Rees; BeyondImages/iStock/Getty Images Plus; Daniel Leal-Olivas/AFP; gbh007/iStock/Getty Images Plus; DarthArt/iStock Editorial/Getty Images Plus; JulNichols/E+; **U12**: Blade_kostas/iStock/Getty Images Plus; mladn61/iStock/Getty Images Plus; Vold77/iStock/Getty Images Plus; Bepsimage/iStock/Getty Images Plus; Nerthuz/iStock/Getty Images Plus; genekrebs/E+; **U13**: mbbirdy/iStock/Getty Images Plus; Hero Images; Onne van der Wal/Corbis Documentary; milindri/iStock/Getty Images Plus; Paul Bradbury/OJO Images; fotokostic/iStock/Getty Images Plus; Blend Images - Jade/Brand X Pictures; alefbet/iStock Editorial/Getty Images Plus; peace!/A.collection/amana images; Suriyapong Thongsawang/iStock/Getty Images Plus; fuchs-photography/fuchs-photography; bowdenimages/iStock/Getty Images Plus; Carol Yepes/Moment; **U14**: FatCamera/iStock/Getty Images Plus; Jovanmandic/iStock/Getty Images Plus; Qi Yang/Moment; Atlantide Phototravel/Corbis Documentary; boonchai wedmakawand/Moment; Image Source/Photodisc; Monkey Business Images/Getty Images Plus; Jose Luis Pelaez Inc/Blend Images; UpperCut Images; Juice Images; Cyndi Monaghan/Moment; Nick David/Taxi; Caiaimage/Chris Ryan/OJO+; bortonia/DigitalVision Vectors; **GR**: Dhwee/Moment; Juice Images Ltd; Hero Images; Dag Sundberg/Photographer's Choice; Frank and Helena Herholdt/Cultura; Robert Daly/OJO Images; Zero Creatives/Cultura; monkeybusinessimages/iStock/Getty Images Plus; RusselltatedotCom/DigitalVision Vectors; bubaone/DigitalVision Vectors; designalldone/DigitalVision Vectors; pop_jop/DigitalVision Vectors; jennifer m. ramos/Moment; Imgorthand/E+; Manuela Manuela/EyeEm; Wilfried Feder/Look-foto; SolStock/E+; Phil Boorman/Cultura; Erik Isakson/Blend Images; moodboard/Brand X Pictures; GlobalStock/E+; Benjamin Torode/Moment; Johner Images; **PVB**: BFG Images; Westend61; Eric Audras/Onoky; kali9/E+; **WB**: Aleksander Rubtsov/Blend Images; Juanmonino/E+; **SB**: Ryan Smith/Corbis; Xalanx/iStock/Getty Images Plus; Marco Bottigelli/Moment.

The following photographs have been sourced from other libraries/sources.

U4: Courtesy of UNHCR; **U5**: Vladimir Vasiltvich/Shutterstock; **U6**: Courtesy of Emily Carey/Curtis Brown; **U9**: Reprinted by permission of HarperCollins Publishers Ltd © 2014 Michael Bond; ©Kung Fu Panda 2008 DreamWorks Animation LLC. Courtesy of Universal Studios Licensing LLC; **U12**: Courtesy of The Zapp family.

Front cover photography by Hans Neleman/The Image Bank/Getty Images; Thissatan/iStock/Getty Images Plus.

Illustrations

Amerigo Pinelli and Abel Ippolito

Audio

Produced by Leon Chambers and recorded at The SoundHouse Studios, London

The following audio has been sourced from Getty Images.

U2: Golden Rule Music GmbH/SoundExpress/Getty Images; **U8**: Short Ton Productions/SoundExpress/Getty Images; Sergey Sereda/SoundExpress/Getty Images; Francesco Biondi/SoundExpress/Getty Images; Pete Kneser/SoundExpress/Getty Images; RFM/SoundExpress/Getty Images; Esther Chung/SoundExpress/Getty Images; shauntoris/SoundExpress/Getty Images.

Page make up

Wild Apple Design Ltd